# The Phenomenon of Untested Sexual Assault Kits

# The Phenomenon of Untested Sexual Assault Kits

By

Darlene Brothers-Gray

**Cambridge**
**Scholars**
Publishing

The Phenomenon of Untested Sexual Assault Kits

By Darlene Brothers-Gray

This book first published 2021

Cambridge Scholars Publishing

Lady Stephenson Library, Newcastle upon Tyne, NE6 2PA, UK

British Library Cataloguing in Publication Data
A catalogue record for this book is available from the British Library

ISBN (10): 1-5275-7330-3
ISBN (13): 978-1-5275-7330-7

The study is dedicated to the victims of sexual assault who have unsubmitted, untested sexual assault kits and to the scholar-practitioners and law enforcement officers tasked with investigating sexual assault. An exceptional dedication to my husband "Nathaniel" for holding down the fort for the past four and a half years and to my kids, Nat and Natalie, who say, "Mom has set the bar high." I also want to send a special dedication to the late "C.G. the Great" for giving me the stamina and wherewithal to do anything to which I set my mind.

# TABLE OF CONTENTS

# LIST OF TABLES

# ABSTRACT

The purpose of the qualitative research study was to examine the perceptions of university law enforcement officials on unsubmitted and untested sexual assault kits (SAKs). Sexual assault nurse examiners use SAKs to collect evidence from sexual assault victims and pass them to law enforcement officials; however, many SAKS remain unsubmitted and untested once in police custody. Without such evidence, law enforcement officials cannot apprehend perpetrators of sexual assault. Sexual assault is a problem worldwide, including on university campuses where there are higher rates of sexual assault than in the general population. The generic qualitative inquiry study was the means of exploring why many officials do not test SAKs in police custody and to assess the perceptions of ten university police officers in two Middle Atlantic university police departments regarding unsubmitted and untested SAKs. Semi-structured interviews, conducted in person, digitally recorded, and transcribed, elicited the experiences of the law enforcement officers. Following the interviews, thematic analysis (i.e., inductive analysis) was the approach used to analyze the data, from which four thematic categories emerged: (a) finances, (b) resources, (c) manpower, and (d) reoccurrence. The research shows that the provision of resources, finances, and manpower is necessary to reduce single and reoccurring sexual assault crimes and to promote the proper functions of the criminal justice system, collective engagement of members of society, and equal value of its citizens, regardless of gender. The study indicated the need for stakeholders to collectively engage, acknowledge the systemic gaps, and provide resolution so that officials properly utilize SAKs to apprehend offenders and empower victims to live healthy and functional lives.

# ACKNOWLEDGMENTS

I would like to acknowledge several individuals who have significantly contributed to the study. First, my mentor, Dr. Ron Wallace, who guided and inspired me every step of the way. A special thank you to my committee members, Dr. Stephen Verrill and Dr. Rebecca Paynich, for the valuable feedback. Finally, I would also like to acknowledge my colleagues: Dr. Johnny Rice, II, for a worthy, relevant topic suggestion; Dr. Ryan Shropshire and Dr. Kesslyn Brade-Stennis, for using their keen eyes during revisions; Dr. Malcolm Drewery, for taking a second look at themes; and Ms. Wendy Velez-Torres, for providing guidance with tracking Word applications.

# CHAPTER 1

# INTRODUCTION

Chapter 1 provides background information on university law enforcement officials' perceptions of untested sexual assault kits (SAKs) and their context in broader society. The chapter includes the justification of the study, purpose and significance of the study, research design, assumptions and limitations, and a summary of the study. Also included is the rationale and context for the study.

## Background of the Study

Police officers and other criminal justice personnel members play crucial roles in helping victims of sexual assault regain their sense of well-being and receive justice[1]. The process of protecting victims' well-being begins when sexual assault nurse examiners (SANEs) utilize SAKs to gather evidence, after which police officers transfer the evidence to the crime laboratory for processing. However, a growing body of research indicates that thousands of SAKs do not reach the crime lab for processing, instead remaining in police property evidence rooms[2,3,4].

---

[1] Rebecca Campbell and Giannina Fehler-Cabral, "Why Police 'Couldn't or Wouldn't' Submit Sexual Assault Kits for Forensic DNA Testing: A Focal Concerns Theory Analysis of Untested Rape Kits," *Law & Society Review* 52, no. 1 (2018): 73-105, https://doi.org/10.1111/lasr.12310.

[2] Ibid.

[3] Joshua A. Hendrix et al. "An Examination of Sexual Assault Kit Submission Efficiencies Among a Nationally Representative Sample of Law Enforcement Agencies." *Criminal Justice Policy Review 31*, no. 7 (2020): 1095-1115, https://doi.org/10.1177/0887403419884730.

[4] Andrea Quinlan, "Visions of Public Safety, Justice, and Healing: The Making of the Rape Kit Backlog in the United States," *Social & Legal Studies* 29, no. 2 (2020): 225-245, https://doi.org/10.1177/0964663919829848.

Several regional studies[5,6,7] have shown that failure to process SAKs is a common practice throughout the United States. Campbell, Shaw, and Fehler-Cabral[8] and the National Institute of Justice[9] indicated that in Detroit, Michigan, there are more than 11,000 SAKs in storage, with 8,700 never submitted for testing. Similarly, in Houston, Texas, there are 16,000 kits in police storage lockers, with 6,500 not submitted. Between the Los Angeles Police Department and Sheriff's Office, there are 12,000 untested kits[10]. Investigative reports have shown that officials perform investigations inaccurately or not at all[11].

The victim's involvement in the process is a crucial component in facilitating the investigation, and involved victims thereby assist in efforts of bringing the perpetrators to light and holding them accountable[12,13,14]. While some sexual assault victims opt not to undergo SAKs, most victims do agree to complete SAKs[15,16]; however, officials may not test the completed

[5] Rebecca Campbell, Jessica Shaw, and Giannina Fehler–Cabral, "Shelving Justice: The Discovery of Thousands of Untested Rape Kits in Detroit," *City & Community* 14, no. 2 (2015): 151-166, https://doi.org/10.1111/cico.12108.
[6] National Institute of Justice, 2015, "Sexual Assault Kits: Using Science to Find Solutions." http://nij.gov/unsubmitted-kits/documents/unsubmitted-kits.pdf.
[7] Joseph Peterson et al., "Sexual Assault Kit Backlog Study," Washington, DC: The National Institute of Justice, 2012.
[8] Campbell and Fehler-Cabral, "Why Police."
[9] National Institute of Justice, "Sexual Assault Kits."
[10] Peterson et al., "Sexual Assault Kit."
[11] Campbell and Fehler-Cabral, "Why Police."
[12] Rebecca Campbell et al., "Should rape kit testing be prioritized by victim–offender relationship? Empirical comparison of forensic testing outcomes for stranger and nonstranger sexual assaults." *Criminology & Public Policy* 15, no. 2 (2016): 555-583, https://doi.org/10.1111/1745-9133.12205.
[13] Rachel Lovell et al., "Offending Histories and Typologies of Suspected Sexual Offenders Identified via Untested Sexual Assault Kits." *Criminal Justice and Behavior* 47, no. 4 (2020): 470-486, https://doi.org/10.1177/0093854819896385.
[14] William Wells et al., "The Results of CODIS-Hit Investigations in a Sample of Cases with Unsubmitted Sexual Assault Kits." *Crime & Delinquency* 65, no. 1 (2019): 122-148, https://doi.org/10.1177/0011128717732506.
[15] Nigela Carvalho et al., "The Contribution of DNA Databases for Stored Sexual Crimes Evidences in the Central of Brazil," *Forensic Science International: Genetics* 46 (2020): 102235, https://doi.org/10.1016/j.fsigen.2020.102235. https://doi.org/10.1177/0886260516681881.
[16] Eryn Nicole O'Neal and Brittany E. Hayes, "'A Rape is a Rape, Regardless of What the Victim Was Doing at the Time': Detective Views on How 'Problematic' Victims Affect Sexual Assault Case Processing," *Criminal Justice Review* 45, no. 1 (2020): 26-44, https://doi.org/10.1177/0734016819842639.

kits, causing a backlog of untested kits over time. Officials destroy many of the backlogged, unsubmitted, untested SAKS[17].

Submitting completed SAKs promptly is crucial to the progression of cases and arresting the perpetrator. When officials do not process kits in a reasonable amount of time, there is a greater challenge to apprehend perpetrators and prosecute cases or to exonerate the wrongly accused[18]. Consequently. DNA analysis is the primary factor that affects the outcome of sexual assault crimes.

## The Potential Utilization of Sexual Assault Kits

A SANE usually administers the SAK after an encounter, collecting biological evidence from the victim in the form of blood, semen, and saliva[19,20], with the evidence subsequently submitted to the crime laboratory for DNA testing. The investigative process is the means of identifying culpable sexual offenders so law enforcement officials can bring them to justice. Victims of sexual assault often suffer from psychological and emotional issues due to reliving traumatic events in their minds (Campbell, Fehler-Cabral, Bybee, & Shaw, 2017; Campbell, Fehler-Cabral, et al., 2015). Therefore, submission and testing of the completed SAKs must occur in a timely manner.

Issues that could present barriers to testing SAKs in an acceptable amount of time include a lack of funding for testing, limited qualified personnel members to test kits, and the lack of emotional support for the survivors of the crimes (Campbell, Fehler-Cabral, Bybee, & Shaw, 2017; Feeney, Campbell, & Cain, 2018; Goodman-Williams et al., 2019). Despite technological advancements, such as the integration of the Combined DNA

---

[17] Julie L. Valentine et al., "Justice Denied: Low Submission Rates of Sexual Assault Kits and the Predicting Variables," *Journal of Interpersonal Violence* 34, no. 17 (2019): 3547-3573.

[18] Rebecca Campbell et al., "The National Problem of Untested Sexual Assault Kits (SAKs): Scope, Causes, and Future Directions for Research, Policy, and Practice," *Trauma, Violence, & Abuse* 18, no. 4 (2017): 363-376, https://doi.org/10.1177/1524838015622436.

[19] Rebecca Campbell et al, "Developing empirically informed policies for sexual assault kit DNA testing: is it too late to test kits beyond the statute of limitations?" *Criminal Justice Policy Review* 30, no. 1 (2019): 3-27.

[20] Rachel Goodman-Williams et al., "How to Right a Wrong: Empirically Evaluating Whether Victim, Offender, and Assault Characteristics Can Inform Rape Kit Testing Policies," *Journal of Trauma & Dissociation* 20, no. 3 (2019): 288-303, https://doi.org/10.1080/15299732.2019.1592645.

Index System (CODIS), there is an increased number of unsubmitted SAKs (Campbell, Feeney, Goodman-Williams, Sharma, & Pierce, 2019; Campbell & Fehler-Cabral, 2019). The increased number of unsubmitted SAKs indicates that there is a need to establish adequate crime laboratories to accommodate the increase as well as a need for extensive training for law enforcement officials on the importance of DNA testing and its usefulness for helping victims of sexual assault (Lathan, Langhinrichsen-Rohling, Duncan, & Stefurak, 2019).

## Need for the Study

The purpose of the following study was to determine the contributing factors to the delayed submission and processing of SAKs. A victim of sexual assault reports to hospital, where a SANE takes biological samples as evidence to continue the investigation to ensure law enforcement officials can apprehend the perpetrators in a timely manner (Campbell, Feeney, et al.,2019). However, timelines do not seem to occur, as officials continue to store the majority of these kits stored in police evidence rooms and rarely submit completed SAKs to the crime labs in a reasonable time for adequate processing (Campbell & Fehler-Cabral, 2020; Davis, Auchter, Wells, Camp, & Howley; Quinlan, 2019). The research drew upon the resource dependence theory (RDT; Pfeffer & Salancik, 1978) to explore the problem of unsubmitted SAKs to advance the underlying behavioral issues of the concern. The RDT was an applicable theory for the study, as the theory provided the participating law enforcement officers to give their perceptions of the misutilization of untested SAKs.

## Purpose of the Study

The purpose of the study was to examine university law enforcement officials' perceptions of unsubmitted and untested SAKs. The lack of processing completed SAKs is a United States–wide phenomenon that presents obstacles to providing justice to sexual assault victims (Campbell & Fehler-Cabral, 2020; Carvalho et al., 2020; Davis et al., 2019; Goodman-Williams et al., 2019; Lovell, Huang, et al., 2020; Moylan & Javorka, 2020). The study was the means of understanding the problem, as the participating officials provided their perceptions on SAKs unsubmitted for DNA analysis (Percy, Kostere, & Kostere, 2015).

The problem underwent holistic exploration, and interviews with law enforcement officials from two university police departments provided the data needed to cultivate an understanding. The results from the study could contribute to discussions regarding why the problem occurs, developing solutions on how to monitor SAKs more effectively to reduce the number of kits in storage. Lastly, the study can provide future researchers with insight into why taking sexual assault cases to court is a delayed (or nonexistent) process or why a challenge to convict perpetrators for crimes of sexual assault.

## Significance of the Study

The study presented a unique situation to researchers and practitioners within the criminal justice field. Members of a particular population of law enforcement employed at two university police departments provided their perceptions on the problem of delayed SAK testing. Researchers could use the results of the study to discuss and explore how law enforcement officers could work more effectively in processing the backlog of SAKs, a prioritization that could occur either by stranger sexual assault cases or by testing every kit. The results of the study could provide the data needed for the research of the origins of the issue and why there are still so many untested SAKs in police storage.

Practitioners can use the results of the study as evidence of the need for funding so law enforcement officials can establish adequate programs to help both law enforcement officials and victims. Funding could contribute to generating written national policy and procedures on properly submitting SAKs to crime labs for testing, developing education programs for more crime lab personnel members to test kits, and developing sensitivity training for law enforcement officials and therapists in law enforcement counseling departments to help victims of sexual assault with trauma. Funding could also provide for upgrading technology for police departments so that when department officials submit DNA for CODIS and find a potential match, the requesting law enforcement officials could immediately access the requested information.

The study could be a means of broadening RDT (Pfeffer & Salancik, 1978) by providing additional information about the procedures for testing. Consequently, the study's results show additional information on the RDT with descriptions of real-world experiences from the participants. Proponents of RDT support the notion that organizations that receive funding for special projects are more likely to have members who adopt the project once finished than are organizations that do not receive funding.

RDT (Pfeffer & Salancik, 1978) indicates that members of an organization need and respond to the situation for continuity (Giblin & Burruss, 2009). In regard to the study, RDT was a means for explaining the negligence in police culture as to why law enforcement officers do not submit SAKs to crime laboratories in a timely manner for DNA processing. In addition, RDT indicates that providers of resources can make demands of the organization, depending on the resource, and that there is a need for critical resources to ensure organizational survival.

The results from the study could influence the law enforcement community by providing an understanding and a rationale as to why law enforcement officials do not test SAKs. The study could also affect policymakers and law enforcement officials by providing knowledge as to why they should introduce, adopt, enforce, or change policies on the timeline of processing the evidence from SAKs. Finally, based on the findings, the study may provide a roadmap for future researchers seeking to extend the scope of the problem of untested SAKs and the continuous challenges that untested SAKs present to the law enforcement community.

## Research Questions

The purpose of the generic qualitative inquiry was to examine the perceptions of law enforcement officials on unsubmitted and untested SAKs for DNA analysis. The study had the following research questions:

**RQ1:** What are university law enforcement officials' perceptions of unsubmitted SAKs?

**RQ2:** What are university law enforcement officials' perceptions of untested SAKs?

**RQ3**: What are university law enforcement officials' perceptions of barriers that could cause processing delays of SAKs?

**RQ4:** What are university law enforcement officials' perceptions of victim notification when their kits have not been submitted?

**RQ5:** What are university law enforcement officials' perceptions of the impact of unsubmitted and untested SAKs on offender accountability?

## Definition of Terms

**Backlog.** Crime scene evidence such as a SAK, rape victims clothing that remain untested after being submitted to a crime laboratory (National Institute of Justice, 2015).

**Perceptions.** Indicate (a) established procedures that are used to make sense of stimuli by the five senses (sight, sound, smell, taste, and touch); the interpretation of sensations is the perception. (b) In Psychology, perception refers to the detection of sensory information from the outside environment and process this information into a conscious experience (Qiong, 2017).

**Sexual assault.** Any type of sexual contact or behavior that occurs without the explicit consent of the recipient. The definition of sexual assault includes forced sexual activities such as forced sexual intercourse, forcible sodomy, child molestation, incest, fondling, and attempted rape (U.S. Department of Justice, 2018). Sexual assault also consists of "intentional touching, either directly or through the clothing, of the genitalia, anus, groin, breast, inner thigh, or buttocks of any person without his or her consent or of a person unable to consent or refuse" (U.S. Department of Justice, 2018, n.p.).

**Sexual assault kits (SAKs).** A container (e.g., box or envelope) of items used by medical personnel members to collect, package, and preserve items holding potential evidentiary value for a criminal investigation (National Institute of Justice, 2015). Also known as rape kits.

**Sexual assault nurse examiner (SANE).** Is a nurse who is qualified to specifically examine victims of a sexual assault by collecting the victim's comprehensive medical history, examining the injuries, recording and gathering any biological and physical evidence (National Institute of Justice, 2015).

**Untested.** A SAK (or other evidence) at a crime lab that has not yet undergone forensic testing (National Institute of Justice, 2015).

**University law enforcement officials.** Sworn police officers employed by a college or university to protect the campus and surrounding areas containing people who live on, work on, and visit the campus (Sandhu, 2019).

**Unsubmitted.** A SAK (or other biological or physical evidence) in law enforcement safekeeping that has not been tested at the crime laboratory (National Institute of Justice, 2015).

## Research Design

The generic qualitative inquiry design was the means used to gather and subsequently analyze the data of the perceptions of university law enforcement officials of unsubmitted, untested SAKs. The methodology and design are appropriate approaches for research conducted to gain an understanding of reasons, rationales, motivations, and perceptions (Percy et al., 2015), as with the study. Unlike phenomenology, grounded theory, and ethnography, the generic qualitative design "is not guided by an explicit or established set of philosophic assumptions" (Caelli, Ray, & Mill, 2003, p. 4). Researchers who use the generic qualitative approach embrace aspects of other research designs and do not strictly adhere to one approach. Generic qualitative inquiry provides the structure and flexibility required for the study, which was a means of measuring the perceptions of university law enforcement officers of unsubmitted and untested SAKs (Kahlke, 2014; Richards & Morse, 2007).

Conversely, the quantitative method was inappropriate for the study. Quantitative researchers collect information in the form of statistics or percentages (Brinkmann & Kvale, 2017). There were no statistical, mathematical, or computational data of observable phenomena collected for the study of university police officers' perceptions of unsubmitted and untested SAKs through the use of interviews (Mertens, 2014). As a result, the qualitative method was the research design used to conduct the study.

More specifically, the generic qualitative inquiry study was conducted in a scholarly manner consistent with other researchers to investigate opinions, attitudes, and beliefs of the participants' experiences (cf. Percy et al., 2015). A blend of methodologies may form something new due to the interpretative nature. The generic qualitative inquiry was the approach used for the study because it provided the opportunity to use open-ended questions during interviews with members of law enforcement, offering insight into the issue of unsubmitted and untested SAKs.

Other qualitative approaches were not suitable due to the strict bounding, definitions, or assumptions of those designs. Phenomenology would restrict the study to researching the law enforcement officers' lived experiences of law enforcement, which was not the sole aim of the study (Moustakas, 1994). Grounded theory was not an applicable design because the purpose of the research was not the development of a theory but rather the use of existing theory (Glaser, 1978). Lastly, the narrative design was not an appropriate approach because the data presentation was not in a sequential manner (Connelly & Clandinin, 1990). The exclusion of these qualitative research designs indicated the relevance and appropriateness of generic qualitative inquiry. Generic qualitative inquiry because of the lack of strict qualitative boundaries and provided the opportunity to construct meaning from the perceptions of the law enforcement participants.

The qualitative study included the use of open-ended questions administered in-depth interviews with members of law enforcement officials to provide insight into the issue of unsubmitted and untested SAKs. The process allows participants to express their perceptions on unsubmitted, untested SAKs. Bracketing was the means used to enhance validity. Tufford and Newman (2012) contended that bracketing is a method for lessening the hidden, preconceived notions that can adversely affect the research process due to the connection between the two. Researchers conduct bracketing to set their opinions aside and become more engaged in participants' perceptions. Moreover, other studies that have utilized generic qualitative inquiry and law enforcement are (Fallik, Deuchar, Crichlow, & Hodges, 2020; Oktavina, 2020; Anasti, 2020).

## Assumptions and Limitations

Assumptions are beliefs that are not validated but accepted as truth (Rahi, 2017). Assumptions can be general methodological, theoretical, or topic specific. Overall, assumptions and limitations are critical components to the advancement of a study. A misstep in identifying the assumptions and limitations could cause bias and affect the outcome. Therefore, any assumptions and limitations must be identified before conducting interviews and analyzing data to avoid misconceptions toward participants' feedback. The subsequent section will present the study's assumptions.

## General Methodological Assumptions

The general methodological assumption is that the nature of reality is individual, resulting in a range of numerous experiences (Rahi, 2017). The expectation was that each university law enforcement official had distinctive experiences with and beliefs about untested SAKs. The second methodological assumption was that, despite the potential for bias, the data collection and analysis was from an unbiased position. Although the assumption of setting aside researcher bias extends across all methods, bias is a particularly relevant assumption for qualitative researchers, including those with a generic qualitative inquiry design. Qualitative research contains a collectively constructed and individual reality experiences and environments (Creswell, 2013, 2014). Additionally, qualitative research requires the collection and analysis of consistent data in an ethical manner (Merriam, 2009). Accordingly, the axiological assumption was made that impartially has worth and included mechanisms to minimize bias in the process of gathering and reporting information from university law enforcement officers.

Another general methodological assumption was that the participants would voluntarily and authentically participate in the study, providing honest responses to the interview questions. To address the assumption, incentives were provided to willing participants. A variety of communication tools was used to elicit honest responses from the participants (e.g., telephone calls, e-mails, introductory letters, consent forms, and Institutional Review Board [IRB] approval information) to alleviate concerns and ensure the legitimacy of the research. These approaches to the research, combined with the researcher's personal strengths and sincere interest in the topic, were the means of garnering voluntary, authentic participation.

The fourth assumption was that qualitative methodology was the best means for capturing the participants' experiences and perceptions and putting them into words (Creswell, 2013, 2014). The study was designed to gather ontological data about university law enforcement officers' perceptions of unsubmitted and untested SAKs. Accordingly, an assumption was that qualitative methodology best aligned with these goals. One final general methodological assumption was that the connection to epistemology, which presents the expression of knowledge as accurate ideas (Walton & Zhang, 2013). Epistemologically, an analysis of the connection between SAKs and how university law enforcement officials believe themselves to be using qualitative methods was incorporated.

## Theoretical Assumptions

The study had several theoretical assumptions. The first assumption was that feminist theory, RDT, and functionalism theory incorporate similar individual assumptions. The thought was that the assumptions of each theory did not affect the inherent value that each theory has in providing a collective framework for conducting the research. Some of those theoretical assumptions were that each person has inherent worth regardless of gender, uncertainty clouds resource-based decisions and collaborations, and society functions best collectively with individual contributors.

Another theoretical assumption was that awareness is a facilitator for change. The assumption was that the university law enforcement officers of unsubmitted and untested SAKs would provide information useful to change perceptions and practices about victims of sexual assault, transform the distribution of resources to address the issue, and enhance the function of each component of the criminal justice system so the agency could function to heightened levels with the slightest amount of interruption and in a collaborative manner (Kalu, 2011).

## Topic-Specific Assumptions

The assumption was between there an interest in the large number of unsubmitted and untested SAKs and that members of society believe that sexual assault is an inappropriate behavior within society. A final assumption was to summarize the perceptions of university law enforcement officers to identify the reasons why SAKs remain untested (Campbell & Fehler-Cabral, 2020; McAndrews & Houck, 2020).

## Limitations

The limitations of the study included the ambiguity within the implementation of the untested SAKs. The untested SAKs affect the communities of law enforcement, hospitals, forensic laboratories, and victims. Law enforcement officials have a distinctive duty to help and protect the public. Law enforcement officers must safeguard the public while relying upon affiliated organizations in the face of diminishing resources and equipment. If change does not occur, agencies will continue to have the problem of untested SAKs. Another limitation was ambiguity regarding the utilization of SAKs by SANEs. SANEs utilize the kits; what is unknown is *how* SANEs use the kits and whether or not such use impacts how police officers process the submitted kits (Campbell, Fehler-Cabral, Bybee, & Shaw, 2017).

### Design Limitations

A design limitation of the qualitative study was the sample of participants. Despite approximately 5,300 colleges and universities in the United States (Hagan & Lancaster, 2018), the population of university law enforcement officers at two university police departments in the Middle Atlantic United States was small. Due to the small sample size and independence of each university department, the findings may not be generalizable; however, officers of other law enforcement departments with similar challenges may be interested in the study's findings.

## Organization of the Remainder of the Study

Chapter 1 presented the introduction and background information. Chapter 2 will present the existing literature on unsubmitted and untested SAKs. Chapter 3 includes the methodological approach to the study, with a discussion of the findings according to the study's research questions following in Chapter 4. Lastly, Chapter 5 will include a summary and conclusion of the study, policy implications, and recommendations.

# CHAPTER 2

# LITERATURE REVIEW

Chapter 2 presents a review of the literature and an evaluation of the studies relevant to the perceptions of law enforcement officers of unsubmitted, untested SAKs. The chapter will present the theories and information about the research topic. The chapter also includes the methods or procedures used to search for sources, the theoretical framework or orientations used for the study, a literature review with a synthesis of the findings within sections, and a critique of the research methods and procedures used in the sources. Lastly, the final paragraph is the summary.

## Methods of Searching

Researchers provide scholarly literature reviews to help readers appreciate the sequence of information revealed as well as the growth of knowledge within a narrow scope. The Capella University online library provided the electronic databases used to search for literature with keywords, including *sexual assault, law enforcement, rape kits, sex crime investigator, law enforcement, victim, perpetrator, sexual assault evidence, DNA forensic testing SAKs, law enforcement agencies assault kits, unsubmitted, untested, sexual assault law enforcement actions, unsubmitted SAKs, sexual assault kits,* and *perception.* The database searches included numerous scholarly databases and journals, including Academic Search Premier, Criminal Justice Databases, PsycArticles, Psychology Journals, PsycINFO, SAGE Criminology, SAGE Psychology, Science Direct – Social and Behavioral Sciences, SocIndex, Criminology, Violence Against Women, SAGE Journals Online, SAGE Knowledge, SocINDEX with Full Text, *Journal of Forensic Identification,* and *Journal of Forensic Science.* Evaluation of the literature's relevancy and publication date was conducted to ensure the articles provided adequate knowledge of the topic.

## Theoretical Orientation for the Study

The theoretical frameworks used in the study were feminist theory, functionalism, and RDT. The three selected theories have common applications among research in the criminal justice and law enforcement fields. Feminism, functionalism, and RDT indicated if there was a correlation between the usefulness of SAKs in crime-solving and law enforcement officers' perceptions of the dependability of SAKs as resources.

## Feminism and Feminist Theory

Feminism in criminology started in the late 1960s and 1970s as a reaction to gender stereotyping already present in the field. Tripathi (2014) found feminism theories first developed and field-tested on men, with a focus on men as victims. In these cases, facts were based on the gender but not the crime, which was a form of sexism. The sexism in criminology is also a major influence on the punishment received by a woman who has committed the same crime as a man. When officials try men for a crime, they do not consider gender. However, according to feminism in criminology, there are different circumstances for women (Shields, 2016). Many feminists argue that officials largely ignore crimes committed by women, simply because they are women.

Feminist theory indicates that women should receive the same treatment as men (Ogletree, Diaz & Padilla, 2019). According to feminism, knowledge may be inseparable from power because of the controlling power of the male point of view on society (Tripathi, 2014). Men provide defining views on what a woman should be in society and set rules to define women's roles and control their lives. According to feminist theory, women have a place in society, but they have unequal positions to men. If men and women had equal roles and shared power fairly, then inequality based on sex would cease to exist.

Feminism is not a one-size-fits-all theory, as each situation is different. According to feminism, people should rethink both the past and future to empower women as change agents without fear (Hirudayaraj & Shields, 2019; Tripathi, 2014). Feminist theory is a tool for exploring the influences of social, political, and economic elements influence on society. Feminism indicates that gender should be a factor considered when looking at consequences such as oppression, domination, and powerlessness in society (Turner & Maschi, 2015). Feminism is not one monolithic ideology but consists of a range of political and social ideologies and movements for fighting for and promoting gender equality.

The concept of perceptions is related to feminist theory in several qualitative and quantitative studies applied to male dominance, suppressing justice for sexual assault victims, and male stereotyping. According to Biana (2020), feminism was the theory used to consider the perceptions of privileged White feminists dominant in the field. Owusu, Nursey-Bray, and Rudd (2019) identified perceptions as a concept when exploring climate change between women and their male colleagues in Ghana. Although the research was a qualitative study, perceptions were a variable in studies reviewed in the literature (Bee, 2016; Daly, 2019; Duriesmith, 2020; Huq, Tan, & Venugopal, 2020). These published studies present foundational knowledge concerning the perceptions of police officers and SAKs.

## Functionalism

Functionalism implies that all facets of humanity serve a purpose and are essential for the existence of humanity (Agarin, 2020). Functionalism is a sociological theory, a principal-agent theory, in which U.S. states could be seen as the entities responsible for delegating certain limited functions to organizations; in turn, members of the organization (law enforcement) perform duties in a nonpolitical manner for the common good. Functionalism is a normative theory evolved from set standards and norms that indicates how members of an organization *should* act, not how they necessarily act. With only a limited ability to explain important aspects of the legal practice of international organizations (law enforcement), especially their involvement with employees of the organization and nonemployees (criminals, the public), functionalism's attraction is the promise of a better world by maintaining global peace (Sinclair, 2015).

General functionalism also ties into structural functionalism, which shows society as one social order (Laluddin, 2016). Structural functionalism theory is a means to find how to achieve and maintain that order in society. Structural functionalism also indicates how different parts of a social system contribute to the whole through the performance of their functions. Structural functionalism presents an optimistic view of society in which every person of the social structure contributes to keeping the structure functioning. Specific to law enforcement, police officers help to control society or social structure by preventing the individuals who may threaten society. Police officers can perform a positive function in that part of the social structure when they maintain order.

Structural functionalism indicates that society is a consensus among individuals governed on a body of rules based on societal customs, morals, and values and that the work of society's separate parts results in the continuation of that social system (Laluddin, 2016). Consensus is not a natural phenomenon for society. Rather, consensus occurs through socialization, where members of that society must agree to the rules and laws. Members of organizations such as law enforcement support socialization by encouraging individuals to be parts of the consensus. There is a twofold result: the survival of society as a whole through the contributions of its independent parts to ensure the continuation of functioning and socializing members, which instills a strong sense of commitment to society's rules and laws, leading to consensus.

Functionalism dominates the field of law enforcement (Lawson, 2014). Police officers exist in a society constructed by their experiences and shaped by the organization's (law enforcement) exerted (legitimate) power on those less dominant. Research into crime and police has a functionalist approach. Functionalism does not include the notion of power or inequality but indicates acceptance of the status quo without question. According to the functionalist approach, police officers act like muscles to enforce the law in response to criminal behaviors in conflict with the interest of dominant groups. Regarding functionalism with law enforcement, anyone perceived to be deviant is a threat. Lawson (2014) asserted that users of the functionalism theory do not consider that by managing deviance, police officers serve to advance the interests of the dominant group.

An argument of policing ontology gains strength by situating the nature of organizations, because police officers occupy the space and are influenced. According to Thompson and McHugh (2009), theorists such as Weber developed principles about the bureaucracy of work. Weber believed that people make decisions based on future consequences and efficiency instead of habits, religions, and customs. People accept authority, and in turn, establish social stability (Lawson, 2014). Most police services are examples of a bureaucratic organization designed to achieve the objectives of law enforcement through rules, regulations, and procedures. There is a clear hierarchy, and members of the organization have specific duties. Employees wear uniforms with clear rankings, and there is a common purpose (fighting crime) that all employees strive to accomplish. The structure of the organization is such that officers have the discretion is to make decisions. Officers work for the common goal, but they do so in individualized ways. In short, the organization provides the resources necessary for employees to do their jobs (Lawson, 2014).

The concept of perceptions relates to functionalism theory in several qualitative and quantitative studies of hospitals, crime laboratories, and the lack of communication between all entities. Chang and Algoe (2019) used perceptions as a concept when testing the functions of emotion using culture. Perception was a variable in studies that focused on (Chrisley & Sloman, 2016; Steiner, 2018; Susskind, 2018; Swerdlow, Pearlstein, Sandel, Mauss, & Johnson, 2020) using precedence when considering the perceptions of police officers and SAKs.

## Resource Dependence Theory

According to RDT, to ensure survival and reduce uncertainty, there is a need for inter-organizational cooperation. However, little research exists on how members of organizations manage to ensure survival and reduce uncertainty. Socially understanding how organizations operate provides comprehension of the actions of the organization, which is a fundamental context for understanding the actions of group members working collectively to make gains (Taylor, McLarty, & Henderson, 2018). By working together, individuals within the organization gain the motivation and trust to develop coalitions and expand the coalition. The organization's growth results in survival because the group members ensure their alliances are large enough to establish legitimacy and bargaining power, thus enabling them to readily access the resources the organization requires. RDT is a theory used to explain the actions taken by members of an organization to minimize uncertainty while maximizing survival through mergers, alliances, and joint ventures (Taylor et al., 2018).

In line with RDT, resource providers make demands to the organization that requires the resources (Giblin & Burruss, 2009). Members of agencies receiving funding for special projects are more likely to keep the project upon completion of the project than agencies that receive nothing. RDT illuminates a need for group response to ensure continuity. In short, there is a need for critical resources to guarantee survival. As a result, members of an organization or group may perform a needs assessment to determine how to sustain the organization. Resources are physical assets and may be either monetary or material. Leaders manage the environment from within to ensure continuous resources. Worrall and Zhao (2003) examined the use of federal support in the form of grants given to local law enforcement agencies with established policies and practices. Members of agencies that had received the funding developed successful policing programs for the community using the resources. In the case of SAKs, funding could be the tool needed to hire and train crime laboratory personnel and establish sensitivity training for the officers who conduct sexual assault investigations. When an organization needs resources, dependence on another entity for those resources could predict either the success or failure of the organization. RDT was thus an applicable theory to the study because officials at crime agencies heavily depend on funding to process kits. The U.S. Department of Justice and the Office of Justice Programs' Bureau of Justice Assistance formed coalitions to ensure that smaller agencies receive the funding needed to continue to test backlogged SAKs (National Institute of Justice, 2015).

The concept of perceptions as related to RDT appears in several qualitative and quantitative studies. Assessing and controlling resources (Garza & Franklin, 2020) on university campuses can be a task. Crime laboratory staff providing DNA processing are not adequately training (Ciccone, 2020). Jakobsen (2020) used feminist theory to consider the perceptions of how members of firms handle tension over time. Knapp, Diehl, and Dougan (2020) applied the concept of perceptions when exploring psychological contracts with employers. Perceptions was a variable in several quantitative studies (e.g., Deslatte & Stokan, 2019; Fletcher, 2019; Gyurák Babeľová, Stareček, Koltnerová, & Cagáňová, 2020; Zacks, 2020). These studies served as precedence when considering the perceptions of police officers and SAKs.

## Review of the Literature

Chapter 2 presents the literature and theories relevant to the research topic, with a focus on relevant research findings. The five points presented are the methods or procedures used to search for sources, the theoretical frameworks or orientations used for the study, the literature review, a synthesis of findings presented in the review, and a critique of the research methods and procedures used in the sources in the literature review. A summary will conclude the section.

## Scope of the Problem

Sexual assault crimes are a centuries-old societal problem. Although anyone can be a sexual assault victim, there are higher rates of sexual assault against women and specific to the study, women on U.S. college and university campuses than among other populations. Practices for addressing sexual assault crimes begin with using SAKs to gather DNA evidence to prosecute perpetrators and vindicate victims. However, SAKs often remain unsubmitted and untested once in police custody. There is little research on the significant number of unsubmitted and untested SAKs with police officers, particularly university law enforcement officers. The research filled that gap through an exploration of the perceptions of university police officers of unsubmitted and untested SAKs (Campbell & Fehler-Cabral, 2020; Moylan & Javorka, 2020).

According to the Centers for Disease Control (CDC; 2015) National Intimate Partner and Sexual Violence Survey, one in five women has experienced attempted or completed rape, one in six has experienced sexual coercion, one in four has experienced unwanted sexual contact or physical violence in addition to stalking by an intimate partner; an additional one third of women have experienced other unwanted sexual contact, such as groping. There are similar rates of sexual assault of women on U.S. college and university campuses, where one in five women has been the target of an unwanted crime of a sexually violent nature (Foubert, Clark-Taylor, & Wall, 2019). The factors that correlate with those findings include the victim's year in college, the victim's race, the victim's level of ability, the perpetrators association with fraternities, the use of alcohol, and the responses of residence hall assistants (Foubert et al., 2019; Harris, Terry, & Ackerman, 2019; Moylan & Javorka, 2020; Swartout et al., 2019; Van Brunt, Murphy, Pescara-Kovach, & Crance, 2019).

Because of these and other acts on college campuses, the federal government has begun to focus on incidents of sexual assaults on college campuses. The U.S. Department of Education's Office of Civil Rights provided the first "Dear Colleague Letter" in 2011 in an attempt to heighten awareness of college-related sexual assault. The effort continued with President Obama's 2014 development and establishment of the White House Task Force, with the goal of protecting students from sexual assault (Harris et al., 2019; Moylan & Javorka, 2020; Swartout et al., 2019).

Victims who experience sexual assault often undergo sexual assault examinations, also known as SAKs, in the expectation that DHC evidence from the examination will provide confirmation of their experiences, identification of the culprit, and justice for their experiences. Unfortunately, SAKs might remain unprocessed once in police custody. The roughly 400,000 untested SAKs (Campbell, Feeney, et al., 2017; Campbell & Fehler-Cabral, 2018), which indicates the presence of gaps within the criminal justice system related to processing SAKs.

Despite the awareness that DNA provides critical information that officials can use to solve sexual assault crimes by identifying, revealing, and prosecuting perpetrators through DNA matches using CODIS, law enforcement officers might not process such evidence in their custody (Fallik & Wells, 2015). As a result, victims' psychological and emotional scars associated with the event remain, the perpetrators remain free, and wrongly accused individuals maintain the scars of false criminal accusations (Clark, Gill, Sasinouski, & McGuire, 2019; Speaker, 2019). The reasons for the breach in submission and testing protocol are unclear. Some researchers speculate that law enforcement officials might not understand the importance of SAKs and their usefulness for court cases (Campbell, Feeney, et al., 2017; Wentzlof, Kerka, Albert, Sprague, & Maddox, 2019). Additionally, law enforcement officers might not submit kits to their crime labs because their labs might have neither the resources nor the capabilities to conduct testing (Campbell, Feeney, et al., 2017; Crouse et al., 2019). A general assumption is that a lack of funding and the length of time needed to conduct testing explain why officers do not submit SAKs for testing. Based on the belief, officers might only regard testing SAKs useful in some instances.

Despite research on the rates of unsubmitted and untested SAKs, a gap remains specific to the factors that differ from one campus to another. There is also little information on the perspectives of university law enforcement officers on sexual assault and SAKs. The study was the means of addressing gaps in the literature, with the findings possibly easing citizens' feelings that law enforcement officers ignore the usefulness of these kits instead of using them to facilitate investigations and bring perpetrators to justice.

## Sexual Assault Definition

Sexual assault is a global public health problem (Inciarte et al., 2020). According to the World Health Organization, sexual assault belongs to the broader category of sexual violence, which is

> Any sexual act attempts to obtain a sexual act, unwanted sexual comments or advances, or acts to traffic or otherwise directed against a person's sexuality using coercion, by any person regardless of their relationship to the victim, in any setting, including but not limited to home and work. (World Health Organization, 2012, p. 2)

Sexual assault includes other forms of sexual violence, including rape, sexual harassment, forced sexual initiatives, childhood sexual abuse, and intimate partner abuse.

Khan, Greene, Mellins, and Hirsch (2020) defined sexual assault as "nonconsensual, specialized touching (e.g., fondling private parts), attempted penetration (e.g., oral, anal, or vaginal sex), or completed penetration" (p. 140). A panel of experts agreed on the definition of sexual assault as descriptive, gender-neutral acts. According to the experts,

> National surveys use a definition of sexual assault that does not restrict victimization by gender, includes a broad range of penetrations, state perpetrator purpose as sexual arousal or degradation, involves force or the threat of force, involves a lack of consent, and includes various forms of unwanted sexual contact beyond penetration. (Khan et al., 2020, p. 146)

## Statistics

There are staggering global statistics on sexual violence, specifically sexual assault against women, who are disproportionately the targets of sexual violence and sexual assault (World Resource Institute, 2017). According to the World Health Organization, approximately half of the partnered women in Ethiopia, Bangladesh, and Peru reported experiencing sexual intimate partner violence between the ages of fifteen and forty-nine years. A report by the World Population Review (2020) indicated that "35% of women worldwide have experiences [of] some form of sexual harassment" (para. 2). Additionally, UNICEF (2017) indicated that "in one-third of countries, at least five percent of young women [have] reported experiences of sexual violence during childhood" (para. 1).

The national data on sexual assault in the United States is consistent with global statistics. One quarter (Khan et al., 2020) to one third (Thompson, 2020) of U.S. women are the victims of sexual assault during their lifetimes. The National Intimate Partner and Sexual Violence Survey conducted by the CDC (2015) indicated that one in five women has experienced attempted or completed rape; one in six has experienced sexual coercion; one in four has experienced sexual contact and physical violence in addition to stalking by an intimate partner; and one in three has experienced unwanted sexual contact, such as groping. Bisexual women are at an even higher risk of sexual assault (Khan et al., 2020). Overall, these statistics, consistent with those provided by the CDC and the National Sexual Violence Resource Center (2018), indicate that sexual violence against women is an ongoing issue and that emotional abuse is a common problem (Khan et al., 2020; Thompson, 2020).

Men are also victims of sexual violence. There are varying rates of sexual violence and sexual assault against men, but all of the data indicate that sexual assault against men occurs at lower rates. United States national reports are that between one in thirty-one to one in seventeen males have experienced sexual assault, specifically rape, during their lifetimes. Two explanations for the difference in rates could be how men interpret the definition of sexual assault as well as other uncertainties associated with reporting sexual assault and sexual violence by men. Men are less likely to report sexual assault due to shame, apprehension of dealing with the criminal justice system, feeling unsure if the assault was a crime, and anxiety about retaliation. Therefore, while men are also victims of sexual assault, crimes of sexual assault for male victims are underreported; thus, there is inconsistent data on the rates of sexual assault (Khan et al., 2020).

Several populations are at risk for sexual assault, including students in university and college settings. At the university level, 20% to 25% of women and eight percent of men experience sexual assault. Moylan and Javorka (2020) found that one in five women on college campuses have been victims of attempted or completed sexual assault. Attempts or completed sexual assaults could range from unwanted touching via physical force to actual penetration. Female students are at higher risk of sexual assault in their first years at their universities (Khan et al., 2020). There is no evidence specific to first-year rates for men, members of the LBGTQ population, or GNC. Khan et al. (2020) noted that by the time students graduated, one in three women and one in six men had experienced sexual assault. There is a need for more information on sexual assault on university campuses, including variables such as age, race, geographic location, classification, sexual orientation, gender expression, racial and ethnic identity, ability or disability, perceptions, practice, sexual interactions, pre-university sexual victimization, and others (Khan et al., 2020; Moylan & Javorka, 2020); however, statistics showing that university and college students are at a significantly higher risk of sexual assault indicate they are a high-risk population.

Incidents of sexual assault have lifetime adverse effects on victims and their families (Thompson, 2020). Victims, family members, and communities might experience individual and secondary emotional, physical, and psychological trauma that ranges from negative images of self-worth to guilt and physical pain (CDC, 2015; Khan et al., 2020; NSVRD, 2019). Haskell and Randall (2019) noted that sexual assault causes a victim shock and pain, which has an effect on the brain and nervous system. Victims often reexperience the pain of sexual assault during aspects of the criminal justice system, including SAK testing and testifying about the event. Finally, sexual assault has an estimated financial impact of $122,461 per victim over a lifetime. These impacts require further attention, particularly with regard to criminal justice system perceptions, policies, and practices related to sexual assault.

## Sexual Assault History and Relevant Movements

Sexual assault is not a new issue. Some of the ancient sacred writings contain reports of sexual assault; however, records of sexual assaults within the last two centuries date back to 1830 in England (Grey, 2020). Sexual assault was not an acceptable topic to write about in those days, so the authors used codes and rewording to address sexual assault. During the 19th century in England and Wales, newspapers were a vital means for understanding the history of sexual violence. There were changes in the commentary of sexual assault against children between 1800 and 1900.

The 1970s brought a rising awareness of sexual assault in the United States with the anti-rape movement. During the 1970s, rape crisis centers began to emerge (Whalley, 2020), since becoming more dependent on legislative grants to maintain their advocacy and awareness work. Rape crisis centers are unwilling businesses to the maintenance of victim services. Whalley (2020) performed a qualitative study using three years of ethnographic research of a rape crisis center and conducting forty interviews. The purpose was to show how leaders of one state's government facilitated a rape crisis center into becoming a prison. The revolution of the rape crisis center enlightened a reply of an enticement and modification to aid the prison. Whalley found commonalities in subcontracting the hotline to criminal-legal victim services, noting that the integration did not expand the rape crisis center and that it was easy to ban victims.

The results were the legal integration of criminals, the development of the prison into a rape crisis center, and the harm to victims of sexual assault. Since the advent of the rape reform movement in the 1970s to the 1980s, cases of sexual assault produced more convictions within the criminal justice system (Spohn & Tellis, 2019). The early effort to raise awareness of sexual assault in the United States was the foundation for continuing attention on sexual assault. The relationship shifted between the centers and the state governments, which led to a connection between the centers and the criminal justice and prison systems.

These early cases and movements in U.S. history also provided a framework for contemporary feminist empowerment and movements such as #MeToo. #MeToo is a growing movement of feminists who use technology and the digital age to fight for equality. Hashtag feminism is the present-day use of hashtags to protest against social issues with a negative impact on women. The hashtag #MeToo, along with several others (e.g., #SayHerName, #WhyIStayed, #YesAllWomen, etc.), provides a platform for responding to public misunderstanding or complacency about violence toward women (Lang, 2019). Although #MeToo has a similar path as some of the other hashtags, #MeToo is a different movement in that participants work against disembodiment of information by presenting the experiences of women who have experienced sexual assault and harassment. Used as a means of disclosure, #MeToo provides structural information on how individuals should interpret information. Unlike other feminist hashtags used to develop communities, #MeToo is a formal census in which the users disclose their experiences, share their stories, support others, and receive support. With the shared information separate from the survivors and their experiences, sexual assault undergoes an additional process of decontextualization filtered through the U.S. rape culture.

Civil rights activist Tarana Burke (2013) started the first "me too" movement when she began using the words "me too" in 2006 to relate with and discuss sexual violence with young female survivors of sexual assault. In describing the events that led to the saying, Burke (2013) described an on-the-fence experience in which a young woman disclosed that her mother's boyfriend had been sexually assaulting her. Burke was shocked and reported the incident, much to the young woman's dismay. After the experience, Burke realized the need for survivors to signal understanding to each other without going into detail. For Burke, the version of "me too" is a way to help survivors feel seen and heard while providing empathy, as they take personal risks in disclosing their experiences.

The second #MeToo movement occurred after the public declarations of sexual assault and harassment by Harvey Weinstein. On October 15, 2017, actress and activist Alyssa Milano tweeted, "Me too," after a friend suggested that all women who had experienced sexual assault and harassment to tweet the words to provide people with a sense of the severity of the issue of sexual assault (Lang, 2019). Milano replied to the tweet and asked others to follow suit. In the days that passed, celebrities, actors, musicians, athletes, and other public figures came forward to share their experiences in the #MeToo movement. Noncelebrity Twitter users also responded to the tweet using #MeToo to describe their experiences with sexual assault and harassment. Fueled by the Weinstein cases, many of these #MeToo participants focused on sexual assault and harassment while at work, but users also shared a variety of experiences, including street harassment and domestic violence (Lang, 2019). Unlike Burke (2013), whose "me too" phrase was a means of building a community among survivors, participants of #MeToo asked survivors to stand up and be counted and to serve as evidence of the scope of sexual assault and harassment (Lang, 2019).

Awareness of sexual assault and related movements in the United States has grown exponentially since the 1970s, with a relatively recent surge of interest in sexual assault on college campuses. According to Moylan and Javorka (2020), there has been a growing focus on sexual assault cases on college campuses from the federal government, starting with the 2011 DCL from the U.S. Department of Education's Office of Civil Rights. President Obama's 2014 development and establishment of the White House Task Force was also a means of protecting students from sexual assault. The federal government's focus on sexual assault on college campuses indicated that there might be unique contributing factors to the phenomenon. However, there remains a need for research in the area as well as criminal justice responses to sexual assault on university campuses.

## Sexual Assault and the Criminal Justice System

The response of criminal justice departments to sexual assault incidents is repeatedly changing. In the 1970s, global and national reformers tried to change the almost-draconian requirements for reporting sexual assault. Before the change, the policy was that the victims had to report incidents quickly, prove that they had tried to fight off their offenders, and show that the offender had used force to make them submit (Pinchevsky, 2016). Reformers hoped that changing the requirements would result in an easier reporting process and that victims would begin to trust the criminal justice system.

Since that time, there have been some positive changes, particularly at the international level, with the creation of the United National Commission on the Status of Women, the purpose of which is to terminate violence against girls or women (Spohn, 2020). Members of the organization actively promote an end to violence in all countries, with individuals in the criminal justice system taking note. With the advent of the rape reform movement, policymakers made changes to the traditional laws on rape that were obstacles for many. The Commission is a means of encouraging victims to come forward and report the crime to the police so that successful prosecution can follow.

Despite changes at the international level, some find a greater challenge to identify national and local changes, based on only minimal change in the criminal justice system in reporting since the early movements of the 1970s (Spohn, 2020). Spohn (2020) asserted that victims still fear coming forward to report crimes, which results in low conviction rates. Individuals in the criminal justice field need to promote policy changes to erase the perception, stereotypes, and myths of sexual assault and sexual assault victims if there is to be change.

Beyond these limited changes, there have been some shifts in policies, including Title IX of the Education Amendments. The main purpose of Title IX is to prohibit any type of discrimination based on sex in any type of federally funded program, including colleges and universities (Goldman, 2020; Moylan & Javorka, 2020). Under Title IX, Title IX is illegal to discriminate against a person based on sex. Title IX automatically provides protection to any individual who feels the need to report discrimination, sexual harassment, or sexual violence. Title IX applies to all public and private educational institutions that receive federal funding in the form of financial aid. Title IX is a means of eliminating gender-based discrimination to ensure that all students have equal access and opportunities in education (Goldman, 2020).

Title IX was originally an amendment created to address and correct inequalities in education faced by women, specifically in athletic programs. However, by the 1980s and '90s, Title IX included other forms of discrimination on college and university campuses, such as sexual harassment and assault (Goldman, 2020). Though there was an initial focus on discrimination in athletics, there was a shift in scope to sexual violence claims in college and university programs. These limited changes indicate that awareness and responses to sexual assault require greater prioritization. Such enhanced prioritization may have an impact on the perspectives, policies, and processes of those within the criminal justice system who address matters of sexual assault, including police officers who respond to sexual assault cases for special populations like university students.

## Sexual Assault and University Settings

University settings provide a unique context for sexual assault. Environmental, as well as relationship conditions, indicate the type of campus environment fostered at the college, including the college's acceptance and response to sexual assault. Research on campus sexual assault in the United States may provide clarity of the aspects of sexual assault in university settings (Moylan & Javorka, 2020).

Tempering the lack of understanding about sexual assault and university settings is the knowledge that there are high rates of sexual assault, especially with male perpetrators and female victims, on university campuses (Holland, Gustafson, Cortina, & Cipriano, 2020). Despite having no clear reasons why men on college campuses act in sexually aggressive ways toward women; however, researchers have identified several correlations between alcohol, athletics, affiliations with fraternities, rape myth acceptance by residence hall staff, and objectifying images of women in media and sexual assault (Khan et al., 2020; Moylan & Javorka, 2020; Wright & Tokunaga, 2015).

A correlation between alcohol consumption and sexual assault is apparent (Kirk-Provencher, Schick, Spillane, & Tobar-Santamaria, 2020). The use of alcohol as a component of campus culture correlates with increased victimization on some campuses (Hill et al., 2020). The risk of sexual violence with medium to high rates of heavy drinking was 1.5 to 1.8 times higher than individual risks at schools with less drinking. Attendance at parties where heavy drinking was an expected part of the college experience was also a contributor, as heavy drinking at college parties is mostly unregulated and unmonitored (Kettrey & Marx, 2019; Nakkash et al., 2019).

According to Moylan and Javaoka (2020), there is a correlation between athletics and sexual assault, as sports may foster rape environments. The athletics environment is one in which competition and winning are priorities, indicating that athletes need aggression to win. Colleges where athletics is a big financial business may have divisions between addressing sexually violent behavior with athletes and dismissing or minimizing sexual assault to avoid media coverage.

Moylan and Javaoka (2020) also revealed correlations between fraternities and sexual assault. Fraternities can be rape-prone environments, as there is an overuse of alcohol, homogeneous group membership, idealization of behaviors of sexual conquest, and the discouragement of monogamous behaviors. In addition, many fraternities have their own houses off campus, which is an ideal setting for sexual assault.

Holland et al. (2020) revealed a connection between the resident assistants' (RAs) perspectives about rape myths and resource provision. Using a sample of 300 undergraduate RAs on an enormous university campus, the researchers assessed the rape myth acceptance, the support provided by the RA, and feminist theories. The results indicated that the RAs who demonstrated strong beliefs in feminism were more likely to pass on resources to sexual assault victims, whereas RAs with a rape myth mentality were less likely to share sources; in addition, who had the rape myth mentality did not provide any support. Thus, there is a need for additional training on the rape myth for RAs and first responders on the scene of a sexual assault.

In addition to the aforementioned correlations and speculations for the propensity of sexual assault in university settings is exposure to media objectifying women. Following surveys and experimental studies, Hald,

Malamuth, and Yuen (2010), Mundorf, Allen, D'Alessio, and Emmers-Sommer (2007), and others found varying attitudes of violence toward women due to men's exposure to objectifying media, including sexually explicit and pornographic material, even without direct depictions of sexual assault (Ferguson & Hartley, 2009; Fisher, Kohut, Di Gioacchino, & Fedoroff, 2013). In a study of collegiate men's exposure to objectifying media of women, Wright and Tokunaga (2015) concluded that men's exposure to objectifying media, even media that does not feature sexual assault, has an effect on men's notions of women as sex objects and attitudes about sexual violence, including sexual assault. In related studies, Ward, Merriwether, and Caruthers (2006) and Wright and Funk (2014) suggested that age, ethnicity, religious status, and sexual experiences may confuse relationships between objectifying media exposure and attitudes toward women. However, Wright and Tokunaga found correlations between objectifying media and sexual assault that remain consistent with prior experimental studies on the direct association between objectifying media exposure, notions of women as sex objects, and sexually aggressive behavior.

The summary of the studies provided insight into university setting factors and sexual violence. All of the aforementioned studies indicated that sexual assault is still a serious issue in the United States and especially on U.S. college campuses. There is a need for continuous research on the issue and the responses thereto.

## Sexual Assault Reporting and Responses

An awareness of the meaning and historical context of sexual assault and the connection with the criminal justice system and university settings provides a framework for discussion of sexual assault victimization reporting and responses. Several studies pertain to sexual assault reporting and response to reporting, specifically within the context of the criminal justice system. The following section presents some of those factors, including victim reporting, police response, and criminal justice protocol.

### Victim Reporting

The literature contains several studies on the relevance of victim reporting and sexual assault responses. O'Neal (2019) showed that a victim's testimony influences the outcomes of a sexual assault case. Other research also shows the significance and difficulty in reporting caused by reliving the traumatic sexual assault experience and the associated criminal justice outcomes. When the victim has to relive the experience by telling the investigator about the assault, the victim experiences second victimization (Garza & Franklin, 2020). The victims might feel as though no one believes them and blame themselves for the assault (Garza & Franklin, 2020; Hine & Murphy, 2019). These internalized challenges could affect how the victim conveys the story, and, in turn, how the investigating officer perceives and reports the incident, further perpetuating the rape myth and whether the case goes to trial (Garza & Franklin, 2020; Shaw, Campbell, Cain, & Feeney, 2017; Venema, 2019).

## Law Enforcement Roles and Responsibilities

Police officers play crucial roles and have substantial power in deciding whether sexual assault cases move on for trials (Garza & Franklin, 2020). In addition to studies of victim reporting, research is available on the role and response of law enforcement. A police officer's beliefs and judgments about rape and sexual assault have an impact on immediate and subsequent responses (Garza & Franklin, 2020; O'Neal, 2019).

There are a few studies on law enforcement officers' choices to query the victims' integrity (O'Neal, 2019). O'Neal (2019) researched the Los Angeles Police Department's sexual assault cases in 2008. The victim's personality and the officer's awareness of the victim's reputation, the victim's psychological issues, the reliability of the witnesses, and other factors affected whether law enforcement officers questioned the victims' integrity and believed their assertions of sexual assault. Similarly, Garza and Franklin (2020) evaluated law enforcement officers' attitudes of crime and victimization as well as their obedience to rape myth. A quantitative study of 517 police officers showed that the officer's sex was a determining factor as to whether the officer believed in the rape myth. There was also decreased readiness to respond to the call when the rape myth was a cognition, compared to a quick response to the assault by officers who had received focused training on sexual assault.

Beauregard and Martineau (2014) examined 350 homicide cases to determine whether forensic awareness strategies were a means of increasing the chances of avoiding police detection in sexual homicides. The researchers examined the use of forensic strategies along with the abilities of offenders to avoid detection in cases of sexual homicide by watching crime dramas. They found that cases involving women who met the victims' characteristics were the cases most likely to remain unsolved. When examining forensic awareness strategies used by the offenders, Beauregard and Martineau found that taking precautions to avoid detection positively correlated with solved cases. On average, police officers identified more precautions used by the offenders when the case was solved compared to when a case was unsolved.

Offenders who targeted sex trade workers were more likely to avoid detection. Additionally, the researchers discovered that victimology has an impact on whether or not law enforcement officials will catch the offender, because offenders who target women in the sex trade may be able to avoid detection. Although the offenders may use several different precautions to avoid detection by studying crime scene dramas on television, some offender behaviors may cause the delayed discovery of the victim, which results in the delayed arrest of the offender (Beauregard & Martineau, 2014). The findings indicate that there are gaps in the literature on victim reporting and police responses. Consequently, police officers have fallen under scrutiny in their handling of sexual assault cases (Campbell & Fehler-Cabral, 2018; Garza & Franklin; Wells, 2016). Garza and Franklin (2020) and O'Neal (2017, 2019) acknowledged the importance of scrutiny against law enforcement and sexual assault case processing for the climate now surrounding sexual assault.

## Sexual Assault Kits

### Definition and Purpose of Sexual Assault Kits

In the late 1970s, within the same decade as movements and sexual assault awareness and criminology, Chicago Police Sergeant Louis Vitullo created the first SAK (Shelby, 2018). Since the 1970s, professionals have scientifically developed the SAKs, which are now accepted tools for providing sexual assault data for use in the criminal justice system (U.S. Department of Justice, 2020). According to the U.S. Department of Justice, Office of Justice Programs (2020), "Advances in the technology for processing and analyzing DNA evidence—plus maintenance and expansion of the national DNA database—have brought about a profound change to the criminal justice system" (p. 3).

A SAK is a collection of items used for collecting and keeping evidence from victims of sexual assault to prosecute the perpetrators (Campbell & Fehler-Cabral, 2020). Medical professionals recommend that victims complete the SAK, which a SANE administers in a hospital in a process that lasts four to six hours. The medical professional utilizing the kit gathers samples from the victim's entire body for evidence (Lovell, Luminais, Flannery, Bell, & Kyker, 2018). Law enforcement officials can use any biological evidence collected for testing to facilitate the identification, arrest, prosecution, and conviction of the offender (Campbell, Fehler-Cabral, & Horsford, 2017; Davis et al., 2019; Strom & Hickman, 2016). Submitting evidence is also a way to prevent future attacks. However, for the kits to be successful tools in preventing future attacks, law enforcement officers must submit them for testing in crime laboratories to apprehend the offenders, and officials must maintain and process the evidence collected to hold the offenders accountable for their actions.

There have been several challenges associated with SAK processing. The challenges include processing protocols, police perceptions and responses, and knowledge and fiscal resources. The next section presents the subsequent consequences of these challenges.

## SAK processing and protocols

After a sexual assault, the victim will likely undergo a SAK examination at a hospital by a SANE. Although medical professionals administer the SAKs, it is the law enforcement officers' responsibility to take the next steps to ensure public safety by using the SAK data to solve crimes and prevent future attacks (Campbell & Fehler-Cabral, 2018). With cases of rape or sexual assault, using the SAK is a way to foster public safety and provide the opportunity to match DNA across crimes.

Although SAKs are beneficial to overall public safety, many kits do not undergo processing in police custody (Campbell & Fehler-Cabral, 2018; Maguire, King, Wells, & Katz, 2015; Pinchevsky, 2016). Failure to process these kits in a timely manner has incensed human rights activists, including victims' rights organizations and feminist groups (Maguire et al., 2015; Pinchevsky, 2016). Members of these groups assert that the victim suffers if officials do not test submitted SAKs, thus preventing the victims from receiving justice (Maguire et al., 2015).

The concerns about the justice system's choice to use or not to use SAKs are evident in two problematic scenarios: one in which police officers collect the SAK but never submit it to a crime lab for testing, and the other in which police officers collect and submit the kits, but the SAKs have yet to undergo testing (Pinchevsky, 2016). Both scenarios show how members of the criminal justice system prioritize protocols of victims of sexual assault.

There is no clear communication as to why officials do not submit or test SAKs. Because of poor communication between the medical provider, police officer or investigator, and crime lab, the media could discover and report about unresolved cases, which could result in distrust of and lawsuits against the system (Campbell, Feeney, et al., 2017). Furthermore, victims never receive notifications of the status of their cases, and they fail to receive justice (Feeney et al., 2018). Additionally, while undergoing the process of collecting evidence, the victims may develop psychological or mental health issues that could cause them harm, as they must psychologically and emotionally relive the sexual assault. Campbell, Feeney, et al. (2017) suggested conducting additional action research with community members who form alliances to address concerns of communication and promote protocol reforms. From a perspective of clinical care, forensic nurses must understand and describe the processing of kits to their communities, subsequently providing accurate information to educate victims so they can make rational decisions about their care (Campbell, Fehler-Cabral, & Horsford, 2017). From a policy perspective, if there is not consistent testing of SAKs, then law enforcement officials must assume responsibility for the submitted SAKs.

Another gap in SAK protocol and processing pertains to the roles and responsibilities of police officers once they have received the SAKs from medical professionals. Law enforcement officers must act with discretion when deciding to use SAKs along with whether to participate in investigations of sexual assault. How sexual assault and related legal terms are defined could have an impact on these decisions. Law enforcement officers, such as police officers or judges, define crimes based on their roles (Campbell & Fehler-Cabral, 2018). Often, these definitions do not present clear processes and protocols for the subsequent adjudications of perpetrators, including processes and protocols for processing SAKs. As a result, after SANEs complete SAKs, there are less defined processing and protocols once the SAKs enter police custody, perhaps due to loopholes in the associated definitions.

Researchers have started to address the loopholes and question protocol for SAKs within law enforcement and the larger criminal justice system. Several studies have shown that law enforcement officers have not submitted SAKs for DNA testing (Campbell & Fehler-Cabral, 2020; Campbell, Fehler-Cabral, Bybee, et al., 2017; Pinchevsky, 2016; Strom & Hickman, 2016). There are 200,000 to 400,000 untested sexual assault kits in the U.S. (Campbell & Fehler-Cabral, 2020; Pinchevsky, 2016; Strom & Hickman, 2016). These unsubmitted and untested kits contain valuable information that law enforcement officials could use to facilitate investigations of sexual assault.

Early studies have shown large numbers of unsubmitted and untested SAKs. Fallik and Wells (2015) conducted a study between 2002 and 2003 of 1,600 police departments with a combined 169,000 reported rape cases. Fallik and Wells discovered that police officers had never sent the SAKs to crime labs for DNA processing. In 2007, another study of 2,300 police agencies indicated that police officers did not submit evidence for analysis. Fallik and Wells thus found a failure of the criminal justice system as a whole because of untested evidence, in addition to a lack of information about the cases and possible outcomes. In addition, they also showed the results that occur when officials screen forensic evidence at a much later date after the investigations have closed.

Valentine et al. (2019) conducted a study using a sample size of 1,874 SAKs submitted by law enforcement officers to a crime laboratory between 2010 to 2013. The researchers utilized the generalized estimating equation to analyze any influences on the submission of the kits, looking at the assault dates and the dates of submission to determine the factors with effects on submission. The sample comprised 40% of members of the law enforcement community and 65% of the state's population. Law enforcement officials submitted 38.2% of the kits. After examination of the kit for the time between the assault and the SAK submission date, the researchers found that law enforcement officials submitted 22.8% of SAKs within the year of the assault and 15.4% a year after the assault because of the pressures of the media and public outcry. The law enforcement officials did not submit the SAKs in the absence of established locations of the sexual assaults. Public outcry and a clear location of where the sexual assault occurred were key factors for determining if and when law enforcement officials submitted and tested SAKs. Evidence of such a high number of untested kits provides a reason for considering law enforcement officers' thoughts on the importance of SAKs.

## Sexual Assault Kit Police Perceptions and Responses

There have been few studies on how police officers view matters associated with sexual assault and SAK processing (Menaker, Campbell, & Wells, 2017). The attitudes and behaviors of officials in the criminal justice system regarding the timeliness of testing SAKs indicate that law enforcement officials may not understand the importance and the usefulness of SAKs for court cases (Campbell & Fehler-Cabral, 2020; Campbell, Fehler-Cabral, et al., 2015, 2018; Campbell, Fehler-Cabral, & Horsford, 2017; Lovell, Luminais, et al., 2018; Peterson, Johnson, Herz, Graziano, & Oehler, 2012). Furthermore, when asked why they did not submit the evidence, the respondents said they were not sure of the usefulness of the kit and that some prosecutors declined testing (Campbell, Fehler-Cabral, & Horsford, 2017; Campbell & Fehler-Cabral, 2020; Campbell, Fehler-Cabral, et al., 2015, 2018; Lovell, Luminais, et al., 2018). In addition, victims who fully cooperate with the police have probable causes to submit the SAKs, which could result in the arrest of suspects; however, the law enforcement officers do not forward the SAKs of victims deemed uncooperative to the DA's office for prosecution, and the cases are not prosecuted. Other reasons for not submitting these kits include whether perpetrators are expected to be declared innocent if the prosecutor does not request testing the kit, or if crime labs do not have sufficient resources for proper testing (Campbell, Fehler-Cabral, & Horsford, 2017; Campbell & Fehler-Cabral, 2018, 2020; Davis & Wells, 2019; Strom & Hickman, 2016). Additionally, police officers may feel hesitant to use SAKs because they believe that forensic analysis is too long a process for the evidence to be useful.

One factor considered regarding unsubmitted and untested SAKs is the age of the victim. Menaker et al. (2017) studied the perspectives of police officers and investigators on decision-making for sexual assault and SAKs. In 2011, the researchers interviewed forty-four of the forty-nine investigators from the sex crimes unit in Houston, Texas, with the sample comprising thirteen investigators who worked with adults and 31 who worked with juveniles. Menaker et al. reached different findings for adult and juvenile investigations. Adult investigations agreed that, compared to other physical evidence, SAK kits provided essential evidence for processing cases. The juvenile investigators, however, said that SAKs were largely unavailable during investigations, and most cases lacked that type of evidence almost entirely. However, when physical evidence was available, those same investigators agreed that SAKs were a crucial component for establishing the victim's credibility, as victim and offender often have different accounts. Adult investigators reported SAKs being most useful for sexual assault between strangers, because in those cases, consensual sex had not occurred. A SAK was an important tool when a juvenile cannot communicate due to age or disability. In contrast, investigators found the kits the least useful when adult victims refused to cooperate or, in juvenile cases, when there was no evidence of penetration. Ultimately, SAKs provide evidence useful for establishing the credibility of victim statements, finding the offenders, and determining if intimate contact had occurred (Menaker et al., 2017; Strom & Hickman, 2016).

Cross and Schmitt (2019) also noted the dearth of research on the response of law enforcement officers pertaining to age of the victim. Cross and Schmitt examined four groups that included adults, adolescents over the legal age, adolescents under the legal age, and children under twelve years. The researchers retrieved the sample of 563 from hospital medical reports of sexual assault cases. Additionally, the authors cross-referenced a database for medical reports, crime laboratory reports, and law enforcement reports. Cross and Schmitt did not find a significant difference between younger or older adolescent victims and adult victims in regard to penetration, genital injuries, biological evidence, and the DNA profile producing a hit in CODIS. Law enforcement officers found the accusation of rape to be false. With children, law enforcement officers initiated their cases with possible arrests. Even though the victims ranged in age, there were significant comparisons between the group members' and police officers' responses to processing SAKs.

In addition to the victim's age, the officers' knowledge of trauma was another factor that influenced officers' responses to sexual assault and SAKs. Understanding the officers' attitudes toward factors that affect sexual assault is a critical aid for the development of policies for trauma-informed training (Lathan et al., 2019). Lathan et al. (2019) found that 21.8% of officers received trauma-informed interview training, and 23% knew about the #MeToo and #TimesUp movements. The officers who knew about SAKs and trauma were more likely to disbelieve the myths of sexual assault. Policy and protocol changes included adding systemwide, trauma-informed training at the police academy so that all officers could receive the education. These policies could be a means of improving officers' responses to sexual assault.

The studies previously discussed provide an understanding of law enforcement officers' perspectives and responses to SAKs. Although law enforcement officers consider DNA evidence provided by SAKs useful evidence for cases brought to court, the officers do not perceive SAKs as necessary instruments for building cases to convict perpetrators.

## Sexual Assault Kit Resources

Resources may be a problem for the use of SAKs. The general belief in law enforcement is that there is a lack of funding and time available to conduct testing, which is Campbell, Feeney, et al. (2017) proclaimed to be the main reason officials do not submit kits for crimes of sexual assault. Although some blame police for not storing, submitting, and successfully tracking SAK evidence, others find fault with crime labs where excessive workload and limited resources obstruct the ability to process and test kits within a reasonable timeframe (Campbell & Fehler-Cabral, 2016; Pinchevsky, 2016). In addition, investigators and prosecutors do not believe that using funding for test kits for victims who may not take their cases to court is a good use of already limited resources (Maguire et al., 2015). Additionally, crime labs already have limited funds for processing evidence.

Campbell, Fehler-Cabral, Bybee, and Shaw (2017) conducted a five-year action research project to determine why there are so many untested SAKs in the city of Detroit. The researchers used mixed methodology to conduct lifestyle observations and interviews with personnel and stakeholders. The authors established factors using quantitative methods to determine if law enforcement practices and policies had any impact on why the kits remained untested. Campbell, Fehler-Cabral, Bybee, et al. (2017) revealed that due to limited workforce and financial resources, there were fewer personnel members who could complete investigations and support victims, as well as inadequate funding to complete testing. Even if law enforcement officers want to follow the protocol of submitting SAKs, the officials do not submit the kits to crime labs if they believe the lab does not have the resources or capabilities to conduct testing (Campbell, Fehler-Cabral, Bybee, et al., 2017).

Both public and private forensic laboratories have the problem of limited resources for processing SAKs. A DNA database can provide useful and necessary resources for analyzing the backlog of kits. Still, because there are limited resources, there should be a return on investment from the jurisdiction (Speaker, 2019). Survivors of sexual assault, survivors of repeated assaults, and measures for preventing sexual assault would receive assistance; therefore, new resources would be available to the criminal justice system. When all SAKs undergo testing, there is a return of 9,874% to 64,529%, which could result in effective policy changes (Speaker, 2019).

Hendrix et al. (2019) surveyed 321 U.S. law enforcement agencies about employment and money contributions and evidence guidelines and how many kits law enforcement officers submit to the laboratory despite having limited resources. Hendrix et al. studied the cost of submitting the SAKs and the lack of resources using the stochastic frontier models. They discovered that law enforcement officers submitted fewer than 60% of the SAKs for testing due to limited resources. Full-time law enforcement officers showed an increase of 24%. The findings indicated that a lack of resources and procedural inadequacies resulted in the accrual of kits.

Summarily, crime labs do not have enough funding to address the testing needs of SAKs. The lack of resources indicates that the criminal justice system views DNA evidence and testing of SAKs as neither a fiscal nor policy priority. These perceptions and the large number of unsubmitted and untested kits suggest that law enforcement officers cannot use SAKs in all types of investigations for sexual assault, rape, or molestation (Campbell & Fehler-Cabral, 2018). Resource limitations, when combined with concerns of processes, protocols, perceptions, and responses, result in the exacerbated issue of SAK backlogs.

## SAKs and Backlogs

For a variety of reasons, including those previously noted, and in many crime labs in the United States, law enforcement officers have not submitted thousands of SAKs for DNA testing (Campbell, Feeney, et al., 2017; Campbell & Fehler-Cabral, 2018; Fallik & Wells, 2015; Hendrix et al., 2019). Although DNA may be the answer to solving crimes of sexual assault because officials can use DNA matches to identify, reveal, and prosecute perpetrators and clear the wrongly accused (Campbell & Fehler-Cabral, 2018), between 10,000 to over 400,000 SAKs remain unsubmitted and untested (Campbell, Feeney, et al., 2017; Campbell & Fehler-Cabral, 2018). Consequently, many cases stall because law enforcement officers do not process SAKs, instead leaving them shelved and untested in police custody for years (Campbell, Feeney, et al., 2017; Campbell & Fehler-Cabral, 2018; Fallik & Wells, 2015).

## SAK Backlogs and Victims

The shelving of the kits results in extended psychological and emotional distress for sexual assault victims. In addition to the painful crimes they have endured, sexual assault victims might be devastated to discover that officials have never tested the evidence they provided (Campbell, Fehler-Cabral, & Horsford, 2017; Feeney et al., 2018). Additionally, the experience with sexual assault and awareness of the unsubmitted SAKs could result in depression, drug dependency, alcohol addiction, suicidal thoughts, and problems trusting the police, among other things.

Additionally, the extended timeframe for testing kits could result in a communication disconnect between the sexual assault victim and law enforcement officers. There are no standard guidelines for contacting survivors, a process known as victim notification, and each city has different victim notification processes (Campbell, Fehler-Cabral, & Horsford, 2017). To contact victims may be a challenge, as there are different victim notification processes in cities and the military. Victim notification could be complicated based on the social arenas in which they live—for example, if a victim lives in an LGBTQ community or a culture-specific neighborhood. From the time of the sexual assault incident to the point of adjudication, several incidents and issues can transpire. If significant time has elapsed since the case closed, necessitating the victim to relive the experience by presenting the evidence in court, the victim might hesitate to engage in the adjudicatory process. Hesitation might also be the case if law enforcement officers have already closed the case and reopened much later after finally testing the victim's SAK.

These experiences, along with limited communication about the status of the victim's case and the results from their SAKs, could create in sexual assault victims' feelings of distrust and cynicism about the criminal justice system. Sexual assault victims hold police officers responsible for the backlog because officers decide whether a sexual assault has occurred and whether to put resources into trying to locate and apprehend the suspect, file charges and, send the case to the DA's office (Campbell & Fehler-Cabral, 2017; Feeney et al., 2018). Although backlogs of SAKs cause issues, some officers believe a kit never turned in will never become part of the backlog. By definition, a backlogged test is a test submitted to a lab that does not undergo testing for thirty days or more (Campbell & Fehler-Cabral, 2017). Furthermore, because there is often no communication between the lab and police, the kits remain "hidden," and employees on both sides do not even know that they possess the kits. The discovery of these kits could lead outsiders to accuse law enforcement officers of impunity. If kits remain in storage and never undergo testing, then the evidence that the victim submitted in hopes of achieving justice does not come to fruition.

## Sexual Assault Kit Backlog and Offenders

The issue of unsubmitted and untested SAKs also has implications for offenders and offender rates. Serial offenders refer to individuals who have committed more than one sexual assault, but the pattern and the number of times they have committed a sexual assault fluctuates. Researchers conducting trajectory modeling studies typically use criminal history records as data sources to model perpetrators' sexual assault convictions; however, they may not accurately show the scope of offenses, as few sexual assaults result in convictions. Campbell, Pierce, et al. (2019) examined criminal history records and forensic DNA evidence from SAKs to obtain a sample of 392 serial offenders, all of whom were suspects of two or more sexual assaults. Using growth mixture models, Campbell, Pierce, et al. identified and validated a four-class model of suspected serial sexual offenders between the ages of sixteen to sixty years. The four classes varied in the overall number of sexual assaults committed by each perpetrator and the ages of peak offending. All classes included sexual assaults identified through SAKs testing and criminal history records, showing that forensic DNA testing of rape kits is a means of identifying suspected serial sexual offenders. Using DNA testing and criminal history searches of identified offenders as standard investigation practices would provide police with a complete understanding of offenders' criminal behaviors.

Offenders' histories of criminal and offender typologies emerged as a result of following up on untested SAKs. Lovell et al. (2020) evaluated the criminal justice records of sexual assault offenders along with data from tested SAKs. The findings indicated that even though sexual assault offenders have lengthy criminal records, they continue to offend but do not commit subsequent sexual assaults. Lovell et al. defined three classes of offenders: high-volume generalist, low-volume offender, and sexual specialist. Several offenders received the label of "generalist" because they had committed many serious crimes (Lovell, Huang, et al., 2020). Unfortunately, the backlog of SAK submission and testing provides offenders with additional opportunities and time to perpetrate sexual assault crimes on additional victims.

## Sexual Assault Kits and CODIS

CODIS connects with the processes and protocols, perspectives and responses, and resource limitations of processing SAKs (Campbell, Fehler-Cabral, et al., 2015; Wells et al., 2019). Before the late 1990s, when police did not have an identified subject, DNA testing was a means of revealing identities; however, there was limited use because there was no database in which officials could compare these samples (Campbell & Fehler-Cabral, 2018). The DNA Identification Act of 1994 proposed a DNA repository bank for individuals convicted of crimes. In 1998, FBI officials established the CODIS criminal database in which a DNA match could provide a lead to identify the offender.

Ideally, CODIS would be a system included in the criminal justice protocols for SAKs. Procedurally, after an act of sexual assault or violence, law enforcement officials strongly encourage the victim to obtain a medical exam and provide samples for a SAK. Licensed and experienced health care professionals conducting the SAKs take samples of semen, blood, saliva, and other materials for DNA analysis (Campbell & Fehler-Cabral, 2020; Campbell, Pierce, Sharma, et al., 2016). After obtaining samples, a law enforcement official takes the kit to a crime lab for processing. Scientists at crime labs examine the evidence for any type of probative value and to determine if it screens positive to extracted DNA samples. If there is positive evidence, the lab worker attempts to develop a full DNA profile. If there is a hit or evidence of a DNA profile, law enforcement officials submit the evidence into CODIS, a database that contains DNA profiles of arrested offenders. If it meets certain criteria, law enforcement officials can load the profile into CODIS (Wells et al., 2019). According to the FBI (2014), CODIS is a means of storing the DNA profile, an identifier for the submitting agency, a specimen identification number, and the name of the crime lab staff member involved in the case. Profiles uploaded to CODIS that match a profile in the database provide invaluable information to a criminal investigator (Campbell, Fehler-Cabral, et al., 2015; Wells, Campbell, & Franklin, 2016). Through the use of CODIS, there have been more arrests and prosecutions of sexual assault crimes (Campbell, Fehler-Cabral, et al., 2015; Wells et al., 2019). Although CODIS is a means of addressing the issues related to backlogs of sexual assault prosecution, there are still relevant issues of SAK backlogs.

## SAK Backlogs and CODIS

The benefit of advancements in scientific evidence in criminal investigations has created a large backlog of untested kits (Campbell, Fehler-Cabral, Bybee, et al., 2017; Campbell & Fehler-Cabral, 2020; Menaker et al., 2017; Pinchevsky, 2016; Strom & Hickman, 2016). For a criminal justice system marred by the large backlog of unsubmitted and untested SAKs, CODIS was the beginning of resolving cold cases when there was the discovery of hundreds of thousands of previously untested SAKs in police property storage facilities across the United States (Campbell, Feeney, Fehler-Cabral, Shaw, & Horsford, 2017; Goodman-Williams et al., 2019; Pinchevsky, 2016; Wells et al., 2019). CODIS resulted in jurisdictions on whether and how officials should test these kits. Some stakeholders suggested prioritizing kits for testing by victim, offender, or assault characteristics based on the belief that these characteristics could indicate the likely utility of DNA testing, a few scholars engaged in research to consider the processes, protocols, and testing priorities associated with the use of CODIS.

Goodman-Williams et al. (2019) randomly sampled 900 previously untested SAKs from Detroit, Michigan. The researchers submitted the sampled SAKs for DNA testing and entered eligible DNA profiles into CODIS, the federal DNA database. Goodman-Williams et al. coded the police records associated with each SAK for the victim, offender, and assault characteristics and conducted logistic regression analyses to test whether these characteristics indicated which SAKs resulted in DNA profiles that matched (i.e., hit) other criminal offenders in CODIS. Testing the sample of previously untested SAKs produced a substantial number of CODIS hits, but few of the tested variables were significant predictors of the CODIS hit rate. These findings indicated that testing all previously unsubmitted SAKs may produce information useful to the criminal justice system and could also be a means of addressing the institutional betrayal victims experience when officials ignore their kits.

The Ohio Attorney General's office conducted SAK testing to clear the backlog of untested SAKs (Kerka, Heckman, Albert, Sprague, & Maddox, 2018). Officials began the project in 2012 and had processed 14,000 kits to date. The objective of the project was to obtain one appropriate profile to run on CODIS to get a hit. The project leads concluded that several variables had an impact on the CODIS profile, including the number of days after the sexual assault that the victim underwent the kit, the number of years to submit the kit to the laboratory, the victim's age, and whether the victim had consensual sex before the assault (Campbell, Fehler-Cabral, Shaw, Horsford, & Feeney, 2014; Wells et al., 2019).

Campbell, Pierce, Sharma, et al. (2016) studied how many SAKs produced DNA profiles that officials could load into CODIS. The researchers included a total of 894 untested kits in the nationwide forensic database. The researchers identified two types of sexual assault: stranger assault, in which the victim had not had any previous acquaintances with the attacker, and nonstranger assault, in which the victim knew the attacker. The results from stranger sexual attacks produced 156 hits on a single profile in CODIS where the offender had fifty-one previous sexual assaults; in turn, the nonstranger attacks produced 103 CODIS hits, where the attacker had eighteen previous sexual assault offenses. Campbell, Pierce, Sharma, et al. found that officials should not prioritize stranger assault cases over nonstranger attacks due to the closeness of the number of CODIS hits for each category.

Lovell et al. (2018) described the submission and testing of SAKs and provided measurements of the outcomes. In 2013, Cuyahoga County's prosecutor organized a team (sample group) to deal with the issue of the collection and testing of unsubmitted kits, along with the number of cases prosecuted and investigated because of testing. The team included members from the prosecutor's office, the sheriff's department, the Cleveland Division of Police, the Ohio Bureau of Criminal Investigation, and the Cleveland Rape Crisis Center (Lovell, Luminais, et al., 2018). The number of unsubmitted kits was 4,373, and suburban police officers identified at least 623 more for a total of 4,996. Members of the team uploaded the kits into the CODIS system, looking for new DNA matches or hits to generate profiles of perpetrators so they could bring sufficient evidence into the courtroom for possible convictions. The outcomes of the study showed the value of using these kits. When officials utilize SAKs in criminal cases, different scenarios result. Through testing, officials can help victims, administer justice to the offenders, and help the community by getting the offenders off the streets. Members of the organized task force discovered that 59% of the tested kits produced DNA profiles that they could upload into CODIS; 39% of those uploaded tests resulted in hits in CODIS. As a result, members of the organized task force added more than 1,000 new profiles to CODIS. These outcomes show the relevance of testing when investigating sex crimes, as the usefulness and utilization of these kits resulted in discovering new profiles as well as returned hits used to reopen closed cases.

Wells et al. (2019) contested Lovell et al.'s (2018) findings because their results showed a degree of consistency across sites; thus, Wells et al. compared two other CODIS hit sites. A slightly smaller number of kits led to CODIS uploads in the Houston (43.0%) compared to Detroit (49.0%), with both cities higher than Los Angeles (35.9%); however, there were similar conditional CODIS hit rates across all sites. Houston and Los Angeles showed similar conditional CODIS hit rates—48.9% and 49.6%, respectively—with a 58% conditional CODIS hit rate in Detroit. The patterns provided valuable information for the researcher, and other jurisdictions in the process of testing previously stored SAKs (Campbell, Fehler-Cabral, et al., 2015; Wells, Campbell, & Franklin, 2016; Wells et al., 2019). The study was one of the first to include systematic measurements of what occurs when officials remove and process older, untested SAKs from storage (Wells et al., 2019). Limitations of the study included the use of a single, large jurisdiction, with a large portion of the testing results beyond the statute of limitations. In testing with these types of cases, the researcher could have observed a variation that exists in other jurisdictions. Also, the researcher could not document the wide range of possible outcomes of testing large numbers of untested kits.

Wang and Wein (2018) developed a mathematical model to predict the number of hits that a DNA profile could have in the CODIS database. The prediction was that there would be a small gain of stranger over nonstranger kit testing, because there were no prior relationships between the victims and the attackers before the attack (Wang & Wein, 2018). A cost-benefit analysis was the means used to test all unsubmitted backlogged SAKs and to test the nonstranger assaults on victims. The results showed testing was a more cost-effective method for the backlogged kits.

CODIS provides valuable information for investigations. Overall, CODIS is an important tool when utilized in the prescribed manner for untested SAKs (Carvalho et al., 2020). Wang and Wein (2018) made four recommendations for departments with large numbers of backlogged kits: (a) Do not test any kits included in the backlog; (b) do not give priority to kits because of the nature of the relationship of the victim and attacker in the crime; instead, test everyone; (c) do test all backlogged kits with preferences; and (d) set the statute of limitations and process and test only kits that fall within those statutes. There are endless benefits of submitting SAKs to provide profiles to the CODIS database, particularly if law enforcement officials follow up on recommendations for protocols and procedures. By uploading profiles and searching for a match for the victim, law enforcement officials can communicate positive messages to the victim and improve their responses on the status of the case (Wang & Wein, 2018). In addition, profiles in the CODIS database can result in more arrests and convictions while preventing wrongful convictions (Campbell, Fehler-Cabral, et al., 2015; Wang & Wein, 2018).

Although CODIS has provided a new opportunity for increasing the number of SAKs that result in convictions, law enforcement officers must know how to use the system effectively. Officers might lack clear communication and protocol for submitting and testing kits, might not have had trauma training that indicates the importance of SAK testing, could work within systems without the necessary resources to facilitate CODIS use, or might have such a tremendous backlog of kits that have been in police custody for longer than the recommended testing deadlines that they feel overwhelmed and discouraged from using CODIS, as was the case in New York City (Wang & Wein, 2018).

## Sexual Assault Kit Backlog and CODIS Recommendations

There are several recommendations for the issue of SAK backlog and CODIS. One such recommendation is a call for law enforcement officers to collaborate with other stakeholders (e.g., officials from the DA's office, laboratories, and victim advocacy) to address the gaps and make recommendations for policy and protocol development to develop services for victims of sexual assault (Campbell & Fehler-Cabral, 2020; Campbell, Fehler-Cabral, et al., 2015; Lovell, Luminais, et al., 2018; Maquire et al., 2015, Pinchevsky, 2016). Officials from the Palm Beach County Sheriff's Office conducted a program to support such a collaboration (Crouse et al., 2019). Officials devised a strategy to address the backlog of untested kits in the Forensic Biology Unit by constructing a consolidated laboratory for law enforcement. The benefits included receiving testing results in a timely fashion, lessening the turnaround time, and ultimately reducing the backlog. Considerations of the consolidated laboratory include the site, structure, employees, and facilities over three years. The criteria examined included the number of samples tested, how long to process, screen, and analyze the sample, and the number of profiles connected to CODIS from the sample. Before the consolidated laboratory, sample processing lasted 153 days, with a backlog of 679 cases. After the implementation of the consolidated laboratory, kits have a turnaround of eighty days. Crouse et al. (2019) recommended having legal counsel for any legislative policies, with all stakeholders meeting in the beginning stages, developing an accurate timeline, and creating an all-inclusive document (Crouse et al., 2019). Successful policies are the key to eliminating untested SAKs (Crouse et al., 2019).

Collaborative processing and policy development are essential tasks, particularly within specialized groups, and produce impactful results for SAKs. Spohn and Tellis (2019) argued that both police officers and officials from the DA's office should make decisions together; independently examining cleared arrest decisions could lead one party to ignore vital information. There is a need to consider solutions for consistent procedures and policies for establishing communication, collaborating, networking, and providing universal policies to reduce errors of impunity, allowing justice for victims and bringing offenders to justice through convictions.

Concerning research-informed policy recommendations (Campbell, Shaw, and Fehler-Cahral, 2018) gathered stakeholders to discuss ways to reduce the backlog. Representatives from criminal justice, the medical field, community, and human rights organizations met with the lead researcher to collaborate on strategies. One strategy was establishing an action research project to develop and evaluate solutions. The project, funded by a grant from the National Institute of Justice, lasted four years. The team members started by testing 1,600 kits, as the city of Detroit did not have adequate funding for testing all of the kits. In addition, the team members developed policies and testing protocol that included case-by-case reviews, victim notification, investigations, and, with the support of the victims, reopening cases with the possibility of arrest, prosecution, and conviction.

Developing a victim notification protocol required discussing the type of approach appropriate for contacting victims, which the stakeholders designed using a collaborative approach. The agreement was that there should be a victim-centered approach—that is, having the victim at the center of all decision-making. Also, the approach should be trauma-informed, which requires monitoring and attending to victims to ensure their well-being and steady support (Campbell, Shaw, & Fehler-Cabral, 2018). The new protocol indicated that officials would only notify victims if there were matches in CODIS after DNA testing and analysis. Out of the sample kits submitted for testing, 455 of 1,600 had hits. If there were no matches, victims still had the right to know what had happened to their kits for emotional closure.

Team members decided that a multidisciplinary workgroup should review cases with hits from CODIS and decide which victims to contact (Campbell, Shaw, & Fehler-Cabral, 2018). All members agreed to prioritize time-sensitive cases. The team also decided that investigators for the prosecutor's office would attempt to contact victims, mostly via telephone, to verify that they had the right person. If the investigators established contact and the victims agreed to speak with the investigators, they would schedule a meeting at the community-based advocacy organization. Both an investigator and an advocate would meet with each victim along with other support if the victim decided to pursue the case. At the end of the meetings, victims received the opportunity to meet with advocates in private, as they could offer the survivors confidential communication that would not leave the area of discussion. From that point, if the victims decided to maintain communication with the criminal justice system, the advocates would act as liaisons.

The results of the collaboration-focused protocol were that the investigators successfully located, notified, and met with most of the victims (Campbell, Shaw, & Fehler-Cabral, 2018). At first, investigators worried that to locate the victims would be a challenge; however, they found most of the victims with little effort. After the evaluations, the team members could put aside the fear about how the victims would react after receiving notification that officials had never tested their kits. Perhaps surprisingly, most survivors did not express negativity after receiving notification, but were more likely to relate disapproval about the length of time that had passed between submitting material for the kit and testing the kit. The disapproval should be a significant influence on testing these kits in a timely manner.

A set of other protocol considerations evolved (Campbell, Shaw, & Fehler-Cabral, 2018). The first was that of creating victim-centered and trauma-informed policies, which required utilizing a group approach to keep the victim educated on the process, informed of all decisions for their recoveries, and focused on their well-being (Campbell, Fehler-Cabral, & Horsford, 2017). Other considerations were the type of outreach protocol, testing, and results-sharing in specified locations and mechanisms with an opt-out option. With the choice, victims could contact a centralized location to learn if officials had processed their kits. These considerations would be a means of notification so victims could receive data and have the right to know any information about a submitted kit while considering that there are some situations where they might not be useful due to the test results and if there is any further legal action with their cases.

Other protocol-related recommendations were two types of sources that collaborating stakeholders and community members could use when developing policies and procedures on victim notification. These were practice-based evidence, where there would be documentation of knowledge of the victims from the practitioners who have created these protocols, and evidence-based practice, where there would be precise reviews of scientific literature with which to identify psychological and legal issues so that practices could be modified to serve victims better (Campbell, Fehler-Cabral, & Horsford, 2017). One question that community members should ask when developing victim notification policies with CODIS is who should get involved. Because victim notifications could have both mental and physical effects, team members should consist of mental health professionals, such as mental health clinicians, therapists, and nurses. Recovering from a sexual assault could take years, and victims could develop depression, suicidal thoughts, and posttraumatic stress disorder. A team must, therefore, be multidisciplinary, collaborating to help with postsexual assault and sexual assault notification recovery.

Miles, Huberman, and Saldaña (2014) provided an analytical framework for analyzing SAK data, with seven assertions: (a) pinpoint a leader of the collaborative group, (b) make sure that all of the stakeholders are familiar with each other and the function of each other's organizations, (c) elect an administrator to deal with inaccuracies and supervision, (d) utilize various approaches for disagreement and involvement, (e) have entry-level members and administrators simplify assessments, (f) maintain an achievable workload, and (g) be prepared for transformations to occur consistently.

The aforementioned reports and studies show support for the concept that members of all parties involved with SAKs (e.g., law enforcement, crime laboratory, hospitals, and DAs offices) should collaborate (Campbell & Fehler-Cabral, 2020; Campbell, Fehler-Cabral, et al., 2015; Lovell, Luminais, et al., 2018; Maguire et al., 2015) to develop protocols and efficiently utilize resources, including CODIS. The literature showed encouragement for employment policies regarding training and technical assistance; also, policy changes within the collaborative organizations evolved, despite there being constant confusion while developing the policies (Campbell & Fehler-Cabral, 2020). Overall, the research indicates a need for successful policies and procedures for reducing the number of untested SAKs and using CODIS to bring offenders to justice (Campbell & Fehler-Cabral, 2020; Crouse et al., 2019).

## Synthesis of the Research Findings

An analysis of the literature showed limited research on the topic of unsubmitted, untested SAKs. There were five main facets as to the larger theme of untested SAKs, the first of which was that the number of unsubmitted, untested SAKs in the United States that have not undergone processing for DNA evidence is unknown (Wells, 2016; Wells et al., 2019). Researchers have contended that law enforcement officials did not conduct DNA testing a decade ago; therefore, a large number of SAKs may be from older cases, which did not receive investigation in the way that officials process current cases (Campbell, Shaw, & Fehler-Cabral, 2018).

Forensic personnel members working in crime laboratories face many challenges with processing DNA from SAKs. Not all kits contain DNA that scientists can use, as the DNA may have degraded due to heat, water, and sunlight (Feeney et al., 2018). Due to the difficulty of processing the evidence, the cost of the kit could also be a factor. There must be valid DNA profiles uploaded to the CODIS database for actual investigation and prosecution (Feeney et al., 2018; Menaker et al., 2017). Along with technological advancements will come lowered costs and faster results.

The researchers discovered that to test the kits was useful for several reasons. When the victim knows the perpetrator, law enforcement officials do not submit SAKs; if the victim does not know the identity of the perpetrator, law enforcement officials can use DNA evidence from SAKs to identify suspects linked to other sexual assaults (Campbell et al., 2017; Campbell, Shaw, & Fehler-Cabral, 2018; Feeney et al., 2018; Menaker et al., 2017; Wells, 2016; Wells et al., 2019).

Over the last few decades, law enforcement officials have begun using and improving DNA databases, as they are cost-effective tools in criminal investigations. CODIS contains profiles of individuals involved in a criminal investigation and evidence retrieved from crime scenes (Amankwaa & McCartney, 2019). Thus, critics are scrutinizing the efficiency of DNA databases and if they are aids in criminal investigations. The research conducted in Houston contradicted the notion and resulted in one case of new charges from a sample of 104 CODIS hits (Wells et al., 2019).

The weaknesses of the system include that offenders convicted of several assaults often do not get convicted of additional sexual assaults because there is a need for a model to track the convictions. Officials collected evidence that contained DNA along with the criminal histories of repeat offenders accused of multiple sexual assaults (Campbell et al., 2019). Campbell et al. (2019) examined the results using the growth mixture model, which they divided into a four-class model.

## Critique of the Previous Research Methods

Sexual assault is a global health problem. Some populations, including women and college students, report significant numbers of sexual assaults; however, there are disproportionately low prosecution rates for these crimes (Thompson, 2020). SAKs are a means of addressing the issue from a criminal justice perspective in the United States. Unfortunately, up to 400,000 SAKs remain unsubmitted or untested, indicating significant gaps in the criminal justice system. Gaps in processes, protocols, and the perspectives of law enforcement officers and effective policies may lead victims to experience continual trauma from the crimes and lack notification, with perpetrators free to commit repeated sexual assaults. Among advancements in prosecuting sexual assaults are the development of CODIS, collaborative approaches to addressing sexual assaults, SAK submission and testing, and policies such as the 2004 Debbie Smith Act for audits and testing and the Sexual Assault Kit Initiative (U.S. Department of Justice, 2018). However, a backlog of SAKs in law enforcement custody remains, along with the subsequent backlash on backlogs from human rights advocacy groups.

One of the gaps in the processing of SAKs is the result of human error. After SANEs conduct SAKs within medical settings and give the completed SAKs to law enforcement officers, there is a breach in practices for the submission, testing, and reporting of the results once the SAKs are in police custody. More information is necessary about why the breach occurs and how the breach correlates with individuals in groups with high victimization rates. Also necessary is to gather information from police officers responsible for the breaches in protocol and practice (Hendrix, Strom, Parish, Melton & Young, 2019).

The research filled the gap in the literature by providing the perspectives of university law enforcement officers. The theories of feminism, functionalism, and RDT indicate that perceptions of women, sexual assault as a crime, and resource allocation may be mitigating factors of unsubmitted and untested SAKs. The aim was to explore the perceptions of university law enforcement officials of unsubmitted and untested SAKs. The study was a means of understanding the perceptions and experiences of the specialized group within the criminal justice system and facilitating the development of effective protocols and procedures for justice for sexual assault victims.

## Summary

Chapter 2 presented the qualitative study review of the existence of scholarly literature on the topic of sexual assault and what sexual assault encompasses, leading to the problem of unsubmitted, untested SAKs. The chapter included the methods and procedures used to search for the sources, the theoretical framework for the study, the research literature, a synthesis of the findings presented in the review, and a critique of the research methods and procedures used in the presented literature.

# CHAPTER 3

# METHODOLOGY

Chapter 3 presents how the study was conducted and the step-by-step procedures and methods so future researchers can duplicate the study. The chapter includes the following elements: the purpose of the study, research questions, research design, target population and participant selection, procedures used to conduct the study, instruments used in data collection, and ethical considerations.

## Purpose of the Study

The purpose of the qualitative research study was to examine the perceptions of university law enforcement officials regarding unsubmitted and untested SAKs. A qualitative research method was the approach chosen and included the use of interviews to obtain law enforcement officers' authentic perspectives without limiting their responses, as might have occurred with the use of quantitative methods, such as surveys or questionnaires. The generic qualitative inquiry approach enabled participants to explore their experiences and perceptions to provide rich data to contextualize the problematic delay of processing SAKs and possible resolutions to the phenomenon.

## Research Questions

The study's five research questions were

**RQ1.** What are university law enforcement officials' perceptions of unsubmitted SAKs?

**RQ2.** What are university law enforcement officials' perceptions of untested SAKs?

**RQ3.** What are university law enforcement officials' perceptions of barriers that could cause processing delays of SAKs?

**RQ4.** What are university law enforcement officials' perceptions of victim notification  when their kits have not been submitted?

**RQ5.** What are university law enforcement officials' perceptions of the impact of unsubmitted and untested SAKs on offender accountability?

The generic qualitative inquiry design was appropriate to answer the research questions, allowing the participants to express their true experiences, including their attitudes, perceptions, and overall outlook of the phenomenon (cf. Percy et al., 2015).

# Research Design

The research design utilized for the study was the generic qualitative inquiry, as discussed by Percy et al. (2015). Researchers use generic qualitative inquiry for research that does not fit anywhere else and to examine individuals' attitudes, opinions, and beliefs about an experience. Hence, the interpretive approach was the method utilized to collect, organize, and analyze the data (Creswell, 2014; Merriam, 2014). The foundation of the qualitative research was the work of Percy et al. (2015). Even though generic qualitative inquiry is similar to phenomenology, they are different approaches. Both generic qualitative inquiry and phenomenology require the use of interviews for rich data collected from the participants. The difference is that phenomenological researchers do not seek to understand the participants' experiences of external stimuli. Researchers who use phenomenology focus on the participants' internalization of the experiences instead of what actually transpired. The generic qualitative study was the means to explore the participants' interpretations of what happens to unsubmitted, untested SAKs.

The generic qualitative inquiry approach was the best choice for the study, as it provided the opportunity to explore the participants' "individual thoughts, attitudes, and opinions, or likenesses on their experiences of things in the outside world" (Percy et al., 2015, p. 76). Scholars who use phenomenology do not probe into the real understandings of a phenomenon; instead, they reflect upon the mental dwelling's individuals use to determine the experience (Moustakas, 1994). The attempt was not to develop a theory to clarify why law enforcement officers do not submit SAKs, the grounded theory approach was not an applicable method for the study (cf. Glaser, 1978). Generic qualitative inquiry provides researchers with the flexibility of not following any specific guidelines (Kahlke, 2014). Therefore, researchers can adjust the methodology to fit the investigated phenomenon.

# Target Population and Sample

For the study on untested and unsubmitted SAKs, the target population consisted of police officers. The sampling frame included police officers serving in university settings in the Middle Atlantic region of the United States. The sample was ten university police officers employed at two universities within the sampling frame (Beitin, 2012; Leedy & Ormrod, 2010).

## Population

The study included university police officers who were twenty-one years of age or older, identified as a university police officer and had six months of experience or experience investigating sexual assaults. Law enforcement have significant roles in SAK processing (Garza & Franklin, 2020) subsequently, university police officers can provide unique insights on the topic as a result, university police officers were an appropriate target population for the study on the perceptions of unsubmitted and untested SAKs.

## Sample

Within the larger population of police officers, the sample comprised 10 sworn university law enforcement officers serving two Middle Atlantic state universities. The sample was purposive. Because there are high rates of sexual assault on university campuses (Moylan & McKenzie, 2018), the belief was that the participants would have insights into the topic of sexual assault and untested and unsubmitted SAKs due to their experiences as university law enforcement officers. Further, the data would provide the rich information needed to comprehend the phenomenon of unsubmitted and untested SAKs (cf. Leedy & Ormrod, 2010; Mertens, 2014; Patton, 2002).

The sample size of ten provided a manageable number of participants without skewing the results. To ensure saturation, five law enforcement officers were from one agency and five were from an additional agency. Saturation occurred when the officers presented no new information. Participant recruitment occurred by contacting two university police departments and seeking permission to recruit law enforcement officers. Purposive sampling was the strategy used to obtain a sufficient sample to understand law enforcement officers' perceptions of unsubmitted, untested SAKs. The inclusion criteria were

- participants must be twenty-one years of age or older,
- participants must identify as a university law enforcement officer, and
- participants must have had at least six months of experience or experience investigating sexual assault crimes.

The sample size was consistent with the guidelines of other qualitative researchers and scholars. Malterud, Siersma, and Guassora (2016) asserted that there is no reasonable sample size for a qualitative study. Similarly, Beitin (2012) and Leedy and Ormrod (2010) suggested that an appropriate size for qualitative research could range from five to twenty-five participants, provided there is thematic repetition. The exclusion criteria were

- participants did not identify as twenty-one years of age or older,
- participants did not identify as a university law enforcement officer, and
- participant did not have at least six months of experience or experience investigating sexual assault crimes.

## Procedures

The aim of the study was to construct meaning from the perceptions of university law enforcement officers to understand their perceptions of unsubmitted and untested SAKs. All of the participants acknowledged that they were university law enforcement officers, which aligned with the target population aimed to retrieve data (cf. Creswell, 2013).

University police departments' administrators in the Middle Atlantic region of the United States received an introductory letter containing the details of the research via e-mail. Two department chiefs provided written permission and copies of their sexual assault standard operating procedures for interviewing their officers. A flyer created included an overview of the study, as well as participant inclusion criteria and the contact information. The departments received the recruitment flyer via e-mail for posting in their break room. CITI program training module for records-based research was completed, and the Capella University IRB provided permission to conduct the research.

After receiving permission from the agencies, a flyer sent via e-mail was the means used to advertise participation within the break rooms. Interested individuals called if they chose to participate. The inclusion criteria were then read to the participant. The participants received a copy of the informed consent via e-mail at least twenty-four hours prior to the interview. Before starting the interview, each participant received a physical copy of the informed consent form for review. Any questions were answered. After reading the information and having any questions or concerns answered by the researcher, the participant then signed and returned the consent form.

## Participant Selection

In line with generic qualitative inquiry, purposeful sampling was the means used to recruit the participants for the study (Robinson, 2014). It was the belief that members of the sample had specific knowledge of untested SAKs for a unique population. Participant recruitment commenced after members of Capella University's IRB reviewed the study's methodology and procedures and granted permission to conduct the study.

University police departments received a letter containing an introduction to the research via e-mail. Open and honest language was used in the e-mail, conveying an assurance of participant and institutional confidentiality and protection (Dixon, 2015; National Commission for the Protection of Human Subjects of Biomedical and Behavioral Research, 1979). The e-mail included the details and significance of the study. Chiefs of two university police departments provided permission in writing. Next, the departments received a flyer that included an overview of the study as well as the inclusion criteria and contact information to advertise for participants in their break rooms. Participants were informed of the voluntary nature of participation and that they would receive adequate information about the study (National Commission for the Protection of Human Subjects of Biomedical and Behavioral Research, 1979).

Potential participants contacted via telephone for more information. Inclusion criteria was read to the participants. The participant provided an e-mail address so they could receive a copy of the informed consent via e-mail at least twenty-four hours prior to the interview. Before the start of the interviews, each participant received a physical copy of the informed consent form for review and was able to ask any questions. Participants were reminded of the voluntary nature of the study and their right to stop their interviews at any time (Mertens, 2014).

## Protection of Participants

Participant alphanumeric identifiers were assigned (i.e., P1 to P10), used exclusively throughout the study to maintain confidentiality.

Identifiers were an additional measure of security to avoid the disclosure of any personal information. All study data, including both digital and physical copies, are protected to ensure the participants' privacy. Upon receipt of documentation from participants, identifying characteristics were removed. Transcripts of interview data from the digital recorder are saved on an external drive, as recommended by Mertens (2014). The laptop, digital voice recorder, completed consent forms, transcription notes, notes, disks, and thumb drives are stored in a cabinet in the researcher's home when not in use. After seven years, physical documentation and permanently deleted electronic files will be destroyed.

## Expert Review

Field testing of the interview questions was necessary according to the IRB. Three experts with PhD's in criminal justice and several years in academia were utilized. These individuals were sent an email inquiry with a cover letter explaining a brief description of the research study and the reason for their selection to field test the interview questions. The purpose of the research, the research questions, and the interview questions were included. The examiners had to assess each interview question for accuracy and impartiality, leading to open-ended questions to allow for vigorous participant response. One expert suggested that some of the interview questions may not answer the research questions. Another expert suggested to add the 9th interview question. All three approved the interview questions.

## Data Collection

Upon reading all of the information and asking any questions each participant signed the consent form. Interviews occurred in a conference room in the two university police departments, and each one lasted approximately thirty minutes. A digital audio-recording device was the means used to record the interviews, with the recorded interview sessions later uploaded onto a laptop for transcription (Tessier, 2012). A pen and notepad were used to take necessary notes on body language, eye contact, heavy sighing, and hand gestures (cf. Mertens, 2014). Storage and protection of the information are in three files, entitled "consent form" (signed consent forms), "transcription" (interview transcriptions), and "detailed notes" (cf. Creswell, 2009; Mertens, 2014).

# Data Analysis

Data analysis commenced from the data collected from individual interviews and was in accordance with the process suggested by Percy et al. (2015) using inductive analysis. All preconceived notions were set aside, analyzing the data from each interview individually. Ten university law enforcement officers answered open-ended questions during semi-structured interviews. The steps utilized were

1. The interview recordings were listened to and a transcript was created that included page numbers and line numbers. The transcript was deidentified to protect the participants' identities, label the transcripts with alphanumeric identifiers. Attention was paid to the participants' body language, gestures, and pauses while recording the interviews.
2. The interviews were relistened to while reading the transcripts to determine the accuracy of the documents. Transcription is an important and fundamental part of the data collection process (Kiyimba & O'Reilly, 2016).
3. The first research question was reviewed, and then read the first transcript to identify and highlight the information provided to respond to the question.
4. Each highlighted response was coded with the letter of the participant, the page number, the line where the comment began, and the research question that responded to, keeping in mind that one response could have addressed more than one question. Coding looked like A-4-12-a. The themes were identified, participant page, number-line of the beginning, and the research question.
5. The transcript was read for the second question, then the third, until addressing all five research questions.
6. The process was repeated for each transcript.
7. Afterward, the responses of the first research question was read to determine similarities and created a separate pile for each grouping. The step were repeated for each research question pile.
8. Each pile was re-read belonging to the first question and checked to make sure of the similarities, adding another for the themes (i.e., the first was 1, then 2, and so on). Each research question underwent the process.

9.  The transcribed interviews are stored on a password-protected computer hard drive in an office filing cabinet accessible only to the researcher.
10. A professional service deleted and scrubbed the electronic data.
11. Coding commenced to categorize data and make them easily retrievable (cf. Merriam & Tisdell, 2015).
12. The participants' responses were repeatedly reviewed to recognize similar themes (cf. Creswell, 2013). Giorgi (2012) stated that a continuous review of the responses provides an impression of completeness.
13. Reviewed responses were reviewed continuously for similarities and differences in the themes (cf. Creswell, 2013).

The identification of themes occurred after reviewing and revising the data to identify possible relationships. The themes were confirmed and well-defined. Reporting of the results follows, with the analysis of the themes that emerged. The interviews resulted in data that consisted of university law enforcement participants' perceptions regarding unsubmitted and untested SAKs.

# Instruments

## General Structure of "Instruments" Section

In many forms of qualitative inquiry, the researcher conducting the study is considered an instrument because they collect the data (Merriam, 2002; Percy et al., 2015). Thus, the credibility of the results depends on the proficiency, and accuracy of the individual doing the fieldwork (Patton, 2002). The interview questions were assessed and approved by IRB. Participants were able to withdraw from the study at any point. A recording device was utilized to record the individual interviews. Innate biases may surface when the researcher is the data collection instrument. To reduce the risk of biases, no personal information regarding the research topic was displayed to sway the data collection and analysis (cf. Creswell, 2013). Therefore, the data was free from any biases.

## The Role of the Researcher

The role of the qualitative researcher in a study is to attempt to access the thoughts and feelings of the participants. The qualitative researcher asks carefully designed, open-ended questions, records responses from each question during the interviews, and transcribes the responses (Percy et al., 2015). The recommended guidelines were followed in the study to capture the perspectives of university policy officers of unsubmitted and untested SAKs. Due to the knowledge of numerous sexual assault cases advanced without adequate processing of SAKs, it was a necessity to capture the real-life experiences of law enforcement officers involved in SAK processing. Due to a model level of experience with research and data collection, it was beneficial to have established guidelines.

Interviews had been conducted before the study for previous employers as a loose form of organizational research; however, the research but had limited experience for a project of the magnitude. Beaudry and Miller (2016) suggested that when there is a lack of understanding and experience in research and data analysis, one must gain experience from research literacy. Workshops and training sessions were attended, and a variety of articles and books were read to develop competence in research methods. As a result, more awareness of the role and the processes of a qualitative study was gained. The interviews were mentally prepared for by setting aside any preconceptions that could have presented obstacles to listening to and interpreting the participants' responses. These were the efforts used to ensure that biases will not introduce errors and prejudice into the generic qualitative inquiry research.

## Researcher-Designed Guiding Interview Questions

Qualitative researchers typically employ interview questions. Semi-structured interviews were utilized for the data collection of perceptions of university law enforcement officials' regarding unsubmitted, untested sexual assault kits. Three field experts who had PhDs in criminal justice with several years in academia guided the development of the interview questions for the research and confirmed their suitability. Based on feedback from one expert, it was mentioned that the interview questions may not address all research questions. Another expert suggested adding the ninth question to the interview guide. The following were the final questions used to guide the interview.

1. Describe your department's procedures for the use of SAKs.
2. Describe past department procedures for the use of SAKs.
3. Describe three barriers that cause delayed processing of SAKs.
4. Describe what would help to alleviate the processing delay.
5. What is your department's procedure if the suspect of a sexual assault is identified?

6.   What is your department's procedure if there is no identification of suspect of a sexual assault?
7.   How are the victims notified?
8.   What impact does processing the backlog have on offender accountability?
9.   Describe what was done about the unsubmitted SAKs at your agency (good or bad).

Each interview question aligned with the broader research questions. The following sections present the alignments.

**Research Question 1.** What are university law enforcement officials' perceptions of unsubmitted SAKs?

1.   Describe your department's procedures for SAKs.
2.   Describe your department's past procedures for SAKs.

**Research Question 2.** What are university law enforcement officials' perceptions of untested SAKs?

1.   Describe your department's procedures for SAKs.
2.   Describe your department's past procedures for SAKs.

**Research Question 3.** What are university law enforcement officials' perceptions of barriers that could cause processing delays of SAKs?

3.   Describe three barriers that cause delayed processing of SAKs.
4.   Describe what would help to alleviate the processing delay.

**Research Question 4.** What are university law enforcement officials' perceptions of victim notification when their kits have not been submitted?

5.   What is your department's procedure if the suspect of a sexual assault is identified?
6.   What is your department's procedure if there is no identification of suspect of a sexual assault?
7.   How are the victims notified?

**Research Question 5.** What are university law enforcement officials' perceptions of the impact of unsubmitted and untested SAKs on offender accountability?

8.   What impact does processing the backlog have on offender accountability?
9.   Describe what was done about the unsubmitted SAKs at your agency (good or bad).

# Ethical Considerations

In alignment with other researchers and scholars such as Tufford and Newman (2012), the researcher showed an ethical commitment to the study by producing unbiased research free of any conflicts of interest. The researcher did not know the agencies or the participants. The researcher conducted bracketing in the generic qualitative inquiry. Tufford and Newman contended that bracketing is a process used to lessen the hidden preconceived notions that could introduce bias into the research process. Conversely, bracketing provides the researcher with the opportunity to engage with and assimilate into qualitative research.

Participation in the study was voluntary, with all ten individuals received sufficient information regarding the study. None of the participants came from a protected or vulnerable group, as per *The Belmont Report* protocol (National Commission for the Protection of Human Subjects of Biomedical and Behavioral Research, 1979). The researcher acted with openness and honesty, inviting the participants to take part while ensuring the confidentiality of participants and organizations (cf. Dixon, 2015). Prior to participant selection and informed consent, IRB approval is required. The participants received alphanumeric identifiers in lieu of names to preserve their identifies. Additionally, all information is stored on a laptop in a locked room in the researcher's home that only the researcher can access (Mertens, 2014).

The informed consent ensured participants would not experience harm during their interviews, and indicated the voluntary nature of participation of the study, and that they could stop participating at any time. Individuals had the opportunity to ask any questions after the interviews. Upon completion of the interviews, the participants received a thank-you along with a $15 Starbucks gift card as reimbursement for their time.

A digital voice recorder was the means used to record the interviews, with a second recorder as a backup in the case of a malfunction. All the written notes, coding sheets, digital files and signed informed consent forms are stored in a filing cabinet in the researcher's home. The day after an interview, the researcher downloaded data from the recorder and transcribed the file. Only the researcher had access to the data. The researcher will destroy physical documentation and permanently delete files after seven years.

# Summary

Chapter 3 presented the methodological approach used in the study, which was generic qualitative inquiry. The chapter included the purpose of the study, the research questions, research design, target population, participant selection process, protection of participants, data collection, data analysis, instruments, the role of the researcher, and guiding interview questions. Additionally, ethical considerations were factors considered to ensure the safety and the welfare of the participants.

# CHAPTER 4

# PRESENTATION OF THE DATA

Chapter 4 presents the data collected and analyzed, the findings, and the results of the study. The chapter includes a review of the study and the researcher, description of the sample, methodological approach, presentation of the data, the results, and a summary.

## Introduction: The Study and the Researcher

Data collection came from generic qualitative inquiry, subsequently interpreted with inductive analysis. The purpose of the interviews was to understand the perceptions of law enforcement officers regarding unsubmitted and untested SAKs. The participants answered questions about their perceptions of the backlog and the phenomenon of the unsubmitted, untested SAKs. Barriers were investigated that caused delayed processing of SAKs.

Inductive analysis was the thematic data analysis method. All preconceived assumptions were set aside and analyzed the interview data individually rather than sorting into preexisting categories. After data analysis was an examination of the emerging themes and patterns from all of the participants (cf. Percy et al., 2015). A synthesis of the data occurred to construe the meanings and inferences of the research questions under investigation. The identification of themes occurred following reviews and revisions to identify possible relationships. The themes were confirmed and well-defined. Lastly, the reporting of the results due to the analysis of the themes that arose occurred.

The researcher was interested in the topic because of previous employment experience as a crime scene investigator working with sexual assault crimes. The motivation behind the topic was that the researcher had seen dozens of SAKs shelved in police storage rooms that never underwent testing, although the victims had cooperated fully in submitting evidence. Due to the experience of working with victims of sexual assault crimes, the researcher could have been biased in judging how long a kit should stay in storage before it undergoes testing. The researcher attended three residencies at specific points in the doctoral program to learn about the methodological approach, data collection protocols and procedures, and data analysis procedures. The researcher has fifteen years of experience as a crime scene investigator and seven years of experience teaching forensic science and investigation.

## Description of the Sample

The target population for the generic qualitative study was university law enforcement officials. The sample consisted of five university law enforcement officers from a university police department and five more from an additional university police department for a total sample size of ten. The officers had to be at least twenty-one years of age; identify as university law enforcement and have at least six months of experience or investigating sexual assault crimes. The sample size aligned with qualitative research guidelines indicating that a generic qualitative inquiry study should have at least five and no more than twenty-five participants (Creswell, 2009; Leedy & Ormrod, 2010). Limitations are inherent in all qualitative research, thus meriting consideration. Data saturation can occur with a sample size of ten participants as long as there is a homogeneous set. The data saturated after ten interviews.

The ten participants consisted of one female and nine male law enforcement officers. All of the participants were Black. The participants' ages ranged from thirty-nine to seventy years. All of the participants had worked for their respective agencies for an extended period and had experience ranging from eleven to forty-seven years. All of the participants lived in the Middle Atlantic region of the United States. Table 1 shows the demographic breakdown.

**Table 1: *Demographic Characteristics of Participants***

| Participant | Sex | Age group | Ethnicity | Years of Service |
|---|---|---|---|---|
| P1 | M | 70–75 | Black | 47 |
| P2 | M | 60–65 | Black | 40 |
| P3 | M | 50–55 | Black | 26 |
| P4 | M | 35–40 | Black | 11 |
| P5 | F | 50–55 | Black | 27 |
| P6 | M | 40–45 | Black | 26 |
| P7 | M | 60–65 | Black | 40 |
| P8 | M | 50–55 | Black | 30 |
| P9 | M | 45–50 | Black | 25 |
| P10 | M | 50–55 | Black | 22 |

# Research Methodology Applied to the Data Analysis

The generic qualitative inquiry centers on the opinions, attitudes, and beliefs within the framework of their surroundings (Percy et al, 2015). A host of questions were asked and permitted the participants to reply with their individual views. Semi-structured interviews were conducted on university law enforcement officials to gain their sole perspective on the phenomenon of the unsubmitted, untested sexual assault kits. The capacity to interview ten participants from two agencies allowed a broadly representative population (Percy et al., 2015).

Thematic analysis was used to pull conclusions. Inductive analysis allowed each interview question to be reviewed and compared to other participants responses. Once the final interview was completed, the comparisons commenced. Problems that arose during data analysis was two of the participants did not have the expertise to answer the questions, so they were unable to provide a response. Meaningful analysis was attained from other participant responses.

# Presentation of Data and Results of the Analysis

The following section presents the perceptions of university law enforcement officers of unsubmitted and untested SAKs. The emerging themes derived from the data were finances, resources, manpower, and reoccurrence. The next sections present the major themes that emerged from Research Questions 3 and 5. These themes evolved from the responses to Interview Questions 3, 4, and 8, all aligned to each research question. Table 2 presents the four themes with alignments to the research questions and the prevalence of the theme.

**Table 2:** *Participant Themes by Interview Questions and Research Question*

| Questions | Theme category | Research Question | Prevalence |
|---|---|---|---|
| Interview Question 3, 4 | Finances | RQ3 | 70% |
| Interview Question 3, 4 | Resources | RQ3 | 70% |
| Interview Question 3, 4 | Manpower | RQ3 | 70% |
| Interview Question 8 | Reoccurrence | RQ5 | 100% |

## Theme Category 1: Finances

The "finances" theme evolved from responses to Interview Questions 3 related to law enforcement officials' perceptions of barriers that could cause processing delays of SAKs. Interview Question 4 related to alleviating the processing delay. Seven (70%) of the ten university officers indicated that university police departments do not have the finances to process the tremendous volume of kits and stay current with processing needs. In discussing financial barriers to processing, participants made several statements.

Participant 2 stated, "I can't think of any reason other than what the media says is money. I'm just saying if there are reasons [for not processing the SAKs], possibly money is one, neglect is another, and incompetence is still another." When probed for any other barriers, Participant 3 said,

> The victims themselves. Sometimes the victim calls, but then doesn't want to cooperate. If they're cooperating, it pretty much goes smooth[ly], but sometimes if they are not in the right state of mind, they don't want to do anything. But usually, the biggest barriers are the victims themselves.

Participant 8 said, "I can only refer to other agencies or my prior agency. Resources, manpower, and maybe policy. There should be a mandate to test all evidence. Coming from an investigator background, anything that is of evidentiary value should be tested." In a subsequent statement, participant 8 provided a broader context related to money and legislatively influenced actions:

> Money and the legislature taking an active role to ensure that the processing is completed would help. The legislature should put measures in place for law enforcement, because everyone has to do certain things to make sure that everyone is doing their role, whether it be the hospital or the police. Any time a victim is raped, she deserves due process. Part of the due process is that a rape kit is completed and submitted for analysis, and then the determination made as to whether it was, in fact, a rape. It would also be helpful to have a suspect from DNA processing. All those things take place, but never in a timely manner. If kits just sit on a shelf and no one does anything about them in terms of analyzing, that's a problem.

Also, other participants noted that finances were a barrier. Participant 1 said,

> I can't think of any reason other than what the media says is money. Other than that, there are none from law enforcements' perspective to answer

your question. . . . I'm just saying if there are reasons, possibly money is one, neglect is another, and incompetence is still another. It could be on anyone's level that someone is either neglectful or incompetent in doing their job, so it could be the nurse, the doctor, the police . . . I don't know. That's just an idea of three that come to mind: incompetence, neglect, and finances.

Participant 5 also identified finances as one of the barriers to processing SAKs, "I would think manpower, money, and equipment. Like I said, I don't know exactly what it all entails when the lab processes kits, but I would assume the more resources you have, the quicker the process would be." Participant 9 described several factors for unprocessed SAKs:

One reason initially [was] the detectives, because it was the detectives' choice whether a kit got processed. Some of [the problem] was funding, and some of it was after the Obama administration, when [President Obama] changed the ruling for more funding for rape kits. The final factor was just not enough staff to get them done.

Participant 9 also noted a positive change and stated,

What was done was good pertaining to finances. [The] police [changed over the staffing. A lot of detectives were moved out of sex offense, and what they did was change the order of processing so that there was a priority in processing. So, all [of the] kits, no matter how old, were [processed].

A third of the participants indicated that the reluctance of the victim was a barrier. Participant 1 said that the "reluctance of the victim to come forward and report the sexual assault to law enforcement" was the number one factor why the kits did not get processed. Victims feel hesitant to come forward for a variety of reasons. Participant 3 added that sometimes victims feel so distraught, they cannot provide anything.

## Theme 2: Resources

The "resources" theme also evolved from responses to Interview Question 3 related to law enforcement officials' perceptions of barriers that could cause processing delays of SAKs; Interview Question 4 pertained to alleviating the processing delay. Seven (70%) of the ten participants indicated along with not having adequate finances, university policies officers perceived that departments do not have sufficient resources to process the tremendous volume of kits and stay current.

In discussing resource limitations as barriers to processing and in relation to finances and manpower, Participant 5 said,

> I would think manpower, money, and equipment [are barriers]. Like I said, I don't know exactly what it all entails when the lab processes kits, but I would assume the more resources you have, the quicker the process would be.

Participant 1 also provided a contextual answer related to resources:

> If victims trusted more. If we as a criminal justice agency could somehow get victims to trust us more. We are not going to embarrass you. We are not going to humiliate or downgrade. That's priority Number 1. Number 2, as far as the police department taking these things and their evidence control, I don't know what their process is. I don't know what their problems are, and I'm not aware of their procedures. I'm sure that they are backed up in their investigations and backed up in storage of these cases, as well. So, I think that our local sister agency has to put more resources into storage, evaluating, and then disseminating the rape kits so that they don't get backed up. Another thing that we have to do is to take these calls and complaints seriously and not try and create a situation where we blame the victim for having something illegal happen to them. So that's a part of training also. We have to train better.

One third of the other participants made similar statements about resources. Participant 5 stated, "I don't know exactly what it all entails when the lab processes kits, but I would assume the more resources you have, the quicker the process would be." Participant 6 found a need "to fix the holes in the system, such as manpower and resources." Participant 8 suggested to "allocate more resources, more money, time, people."
Participant 8 also added,

> Do you have enough people to process to do the testing? What about performing the test? I know that where I came from, getting DNA tested was a challenge because we only had one or two certified people that could actually do the test. The manpower part is you have to have the people with the credentials or certifications to perform those types of tests.

Participant 3 contended that the victim was a barrier.

> The victims themselves. Sometimes the victim calls, but then doesn't want to cooperate. If they're cooperating, it pretty much goes smooth[ly], but sometimes if they are not in the right state of mind, they don't want to do anything. But usually, the biggest barriers are the victims themselves.

## Theme 3: Manpower

The "manpower" theme was the last to evolve from responses to Interview Questions 3 and 4 related to law enforcement officials' perceptions of barriers that could cause processing delays of SAKs and the alleviation thereof. Often along with the obstacles of finances and resources, university police officers perceived that departments and crime labs lacked the necessary manpower to stay current with processing the large volume of kits.

Seven (70%) participants indicated that manpower was a barrier in processing SAKs and nine (90%) participants said that manpower was a barrier to perpetrator apprehension for the crime. In discussing the barrier of manpower, and in addition to the previously noted statements that connect manpower, resources, and finances, Participant 8 said, "Resources, manpower, and maybe policy [are barriers]. There should be a mandate to test all evidence. Coming from an investigator background, anything that is of evidentiary value should be tested." Participant 9 also highlighted manpower, albeit in reference to personnel responsibilities specific to barriers to processing delays.

> One reason initially [was] the detectives, because it was the detectives' choice whether a kit got processed. Some of [the problem] was funding, and some of it was after the Obama administration, when [President Obama] changed the ruling for more funding for rape kits. The final factor was just not enough staff to get them done.

Finally, Participant 2 referenced workforce incompetence as a barrier to the processing of kits. When probed about the source of the ineptitude, Participant 2 said,

> The thing is, I really can't say on anyone's part. I'm just saying if there are reasons, possibly money is one, neglect is another, and incompetence is still another. It could be on anyone's level that someone is either neglectful or incompetent in doing their job, so it could be the nurse, the doctor, the police . . . I don't know. That's just an idea of three that come to mind: incompetence, neglect, and finances.

Participant 5 indicated that the cooperation of the victim was a barrier.

> The cooperation of the victim, the person who was sexually assaulted can be a huge barrier. A lot of times they want to report it, but they don't want to go forward with the process for whatever their personal reasons are. That's usually the biggest thing. From my knowledge and experience, victims really don't push for reasons why their kits aren't processed. When

> I was at [name redacted], the police don't really pursue a lot of these cases if the victim does not want to go forward. They preserve the kits just in case the victim changes their mind for whatever reason, so they still have all the evidence should the victim choose to go forward

Participant 6 contradicted this notion and indicated that the shortfall was on the crime labs side as far as not having enough qualified technicians to process the kits.

> When I said "manpower," I'm thinking about the crime lab unit being short staffed. I know that in recent years, [name redacted] has been very short-staffed. It's probably more short-staffed now than ever, and that has become a hindrance. As for resources, I'm pretty sure this is why. I've ran into cases where we had to reach out to other agencies to help us, such as [name redacted] and that's not even on the sexual assault case side that I'm talking about. I'm talking about when it comes to air support helicopters or units on the street having issues.

## Theme 4: Reoccurrence

The "reoccurrence" theme evolved from responses to Interview Question 8 related to the backlog of SAKs on offender accountability. More specifically, the primary impact identified was the continuation of crime without the apprehension of the suspect. Ten (100%) of the participants indicated that not processing the backlog would have a negative impact and hinder the investigation process. The perpetrators would continue to offend because they had not been apprehended and, therefore, would not be held accountable for their sexual assault crime.

Several officers provided data on the topic. Participant 9 acknowledged that

> With any investigation, the longer the suspect is on the streets, the probability is higher of them doing it again. When a suspect is not caught, they feel they have a superpower, like they can't get caught. It leads to continuing crime patterns.

Participant 6 believed the backlog could cause serious problems for the victims in the long run:

> I believe the backlog has serious repercussions for the victim. The backlog can assist the offender, as the offender can continue to offend if they are not caught. They makes more cases and leaves more victims—more cases where the offender is probably getting smarter and cleaning up his tracks better.

Participant 8 indicated,

> Minimizing the backlog, processing the evidence as fast and [as] thorough[ly] as possible can very well get someone who should not be on the street off the street and into the criminal justice system in a reasonable amount of time.

In relation to reoccurrence and evidence provided by SAKs, there were several relevant responses. Participant 1 connected the presence of evidence with the arrest of criminals, saying, "The DNA and evidence are always going to be there. Once the investigator starts to clear cases, defendants will be arrested and taken off the streets."

The participants reported the steps taken in their departments if the suspect remained unidentified. Nine (90%) out of ten respondents indicated the investigative steps required if there was no identification of a suspect. Participant 2 stated that follow-up was more of a matter for the local police department:

> The police department will now have to do a little more due diligence to try and locate a suspect. If [the suspect] is a student [or] faculty or staff member, we may have more information to provide that [the police] don't actually have because we are already here on the campus. If the suspect is not identified, they will ask us to do everything we can to help, but their position is to interview any possible witnesses and the victim to see if they can obtain or secure who might be the alleged suspect.

Participant 3 shared an in-depth, step-by-step process:

> Take the statement from the victim. Try to talk to witnesses. Try to identify if it happened on campus and find a time block. Watch [the] video for hours, and during that time block from the description that the victim gives, find the suspect.

Participant 7 and Participant 8 listed steps according to working with the DNA database:

> If the suspect is not identified, the only thing you can do is put whatever DNA is taken out of the [SAK] kit into the database—the DNA database— to see if it comes up with a hit. If a hit comes up where it was identified as a suspect, then that suspect's photo information [will] be taken and probably put into a photographic lineup, and that lineup would be shown to the victim to see if she can possibly identify the assailant.

Participant 8 said the objective was "to collect any evidence. Anything that can be submitted into a database such as CODIS to get a hit."

Seven (70%) participants indicated that manpower was a barrier. Most crime labs do not have enough employees to process the kits. Crime labs do not have enough staff, resulting in the backlog of unprocessed, untested SAKs. If officials could clear the backlogs, as nine (90%) participants indicated, they could apprehend more offenders quicker. Participant 1 offered a rational scenario of what could occur if officials cleared the backlogs:

> The more you can process and can clear up that backlog, the more successful you are going to be and have an offender accounted for. The evidence is not going to change, so if you clear that stuff up, then what will start happening is that you will start clearing cases, you [will] start arresting defendants, and ultimately tak[e] these people off [of] the streets.

Participant 6 believed that the backlog could cause serious problems for the victims in the long run:

> I believe the backlog has serious repercussions for the victim. The backlog can assist the offender, as the offender can continue to offend if they are not caught. This makes more cases and leaves more victims—more cases where the offender is probably getting smarter and cleaning up his tracks better.

Participant 8 said,

> Minimizing the backlog, processing the evidence as fast and [as] thorough[ly] as possible can very well get someone who should not be on the street off the street and into the criminal justice system in a reasonable amount of time.

In relation to reoccurrence and evidence provided by SAKs, there were several relevant responses. Participant 1 connected the presence of evidence with the arrest of criminals, saying, "The DNA and evidence are always going to be there. Once the investigator starts to clear cases, defendants will be arrested and taken off the streets."

The participants described their knowledge and awareness of department procedures if they identified a suspect. Nine (90%) participants described the victim notification process. Participant 2 stated that there were multiple answers to the question, continuing,

> If the victim informed us or the police department of a suspect, they will go with that. They will let the victim know that based on the information they provided, the suspect has been identified and we are going with it.

Participant 3 noted that both the campus detectives and local police work officers together and said,

> Once we pass it off to [name redacted], [the police officers] usually keep open communication with me and the detective. The detective will usually call and bring the victim in [after] we send them to our counselor. The counselor usually has close contact with [the victim and provides] other outside sources she might send them to.

Participant 5 had no knowledge of procedures, stating, "I don't know because we don't handle sexual assault investigations. I would assume that a detective is assigned to that case." Participant 9 described the procedure when cases become a year old:

> They should be notified by a cold case detective if it's a case that's over one year old. If that's the case, detectives need to come out and reinterview the victim and do some other things to bring [the victim] in so that the state attorney can talk to them about which direction they are going with the case. If it [had] happened six months ago, the original detective would contact them.

## Summary

Chapter 4 presented the interview responses of the ten participants. The purpose of the generic qualitative inquiry research study was to explore the perceptions of university law enforcement officials regarding unsubmitted, untested SAKs. Thematic analysis–inductive analysis method by Percy et al. (2015) was utilized to analyze the responses from the participants to uncover common patterns and themes. Following data analysis, four major themes emerged: finance, resources, manpower, and reoccurrence.

Chapter 5 presents a discussion of the results relative to the study's research questions and an interpretation of the findings in the context of the existing literature. Chapter 5 will conclude with the practical implications of the findings and suggestions for future research.

# CHAPTER 5

# DISCUSSION, IMPLICATIONS, RECOMMENDATIONS

The purpose of the study was to examine the perceptions of university law enforcement officials on unsubmitted and untested SAKs. Chapter 5 presents the conclusions to the study including a summary of the results and the discussion. Also included are the conclusions drawn from the results, the limitations of the study, and an assessment of the implications. Lastly, the chapter presents recommendations for future research.

## Summary of the Results

A generic qualitative inquiry approach was the research design used to capture the perceptions of university law enforcement officers regarding unsubmitted and untested SAKs. Sexual assault is a significant global and national issue, occurring at high rates within the college and university environment (Moylan & McKenzie, 2018; World Resource Institute, 2017). SANEs and police officers use SAKs to identify and apprehend perpetrators; however, statistics show that approximately 400,000 SAKs remain unsubmitted and untested. Consequently, perpetrators go unprosecuted and victims do not receive justice (Carvalho et al., 2020; Garza & Franklin, 2020; Lovell et al., 2020).

Previous studies of law enforcement officers related to unsubmitted and untested SAKs provided substantial information, including the traumatic impact on victims, gaps in SAK processing, officers' discretion in testing and submission, limited availability of resources, limited to no updated policies other than Title IV, the positive impact of CODIS, and the need for collaborative efforts to address sexual assault and SAK processing. Prior research presented findings for law enforcement in general, with limited studies on university law enforcement officers and unsubmitted and untested SAKs. Literature published within the past 6 months aligned with the study's findings, indicating the need for collaboration to address the issue (Campbell & Fehler-Cabral, 2020; Carvalho et al., 2020).

The generic qualitative inquiry study is a significant contribution, as it filled the gap in the literature by presenting university law enforcement officials' attitudes, opinions, beliefs, and experiences of unsubmitted and untested SAKs. The theories of feminism, functionalism, and RDT provided the theoretical foundations of the study. Purposive sampling was the recruitment method, with 10 law enforcement officers from two U.S. Middle Atlantic universities participating in semi-structured interviews. The officers answered nine prepared questions about unsubmitted and untested SAKs. The findings resulted in four emergent themes: finances, resources, manpower, and reoccurrence.

## Discussion of the Results

Five research questions and four themes emerged in response to two research questions: What are university law enforcement officials' perceptions of barriers that could cause processing delays of SAKs? and What are university law enforcement officials' perceptions of the impact of unsubmitted and untested SAKs on offender accountability? A generic qualitative inquiry method was appropriate to gather and analyze the data. The purpose of the study was to examine university law enforcement officials' perceptions of unsubmitted and untested SAKs.

Data analysis occurred using Percy et al.'s (2015) procedures. Four major themes emerged in the questions: finances, resources, manpower, and reoccurrence. The themes align with Research Questions 3 and 5 and the related interview questions.

### Theme 1 Discussion: Finances

Finances was the first theme. The majority of the participants identified finances and the lack thereof as a major impediment to SAK submission and testing. Officers noted the impact of financial barriers on the provision of resources, manpower, daily operations, and fulfillment of roles. Finally, the officers recognized a link between finances and legislation, which ensures that each entity related to SAK submission and testing has a defined and completed role.

RDT, functionalism, and feminist theories provided a framework by which to view the theme. RDT pertains to a law enforcement agency's need for resources, including finances, to operate and address issues assigned to that agency. The theory indicates that members of agencies receiving funding for special projects are more likely to continue the project even after funding discontinues than are agencies receiving no financial support (Giblin & Burruss, 2009). The findings from the study corroborate the relevance of RDT when considering finances for SAK processing. Consistent with the theory, officers felt overcoming the barrier of finances could assist in the processing of SAKs (Garza & Franklin, 2020; Lovell, Huang, et al., 2020). In summary, the officers noted the need for funds to address issues related to unsubmitted and untested SAKs.

Functionalism, as a theoretical construct, is specific to the purpose and operation of each facet of that culture, showing that each aspect is dependent on the others to supply stability and operation to a whole culture (Sinclair, 2015). Law enforcement, with the responsibility to serve and protect its members while minimizing threats to society, is one component of a larger culture. Limited finances impact law enforcements' ability to provide optimal service and protection. From the functionalist perspective, financial limitations related to SAK submission and testing prevent officers from functioning in a manner consistent with their expected role. As a result, perpetrators are not prosecuted and held accountable for the sexual assault offenses they commit (Lovell, Huang, et al., 2020). Also, sexual assault victims endure unresolved emotional trauma, which might prevent them from further interaction with law enforcement (Garza & Franklin, 2020).

Feminism indicates that men hold defined, often subservient views of what women should be in a society that minimizes the importance of their roles, contributions, and concerns. According to feminism, women should work to establish rules and positions for themselves that are equal to those of men (Tripathi, 2014). Although men comprise the majority of law enforcement officers, including the participants in the study, the crime of sexual assault is one that primarily impacts women. From the feminist theoretical perspective, unsubmitted and untested SAKs might not seem an urgent issue within the male-dominated profession. Consequently, SAK testing might not receive the financial support necessary to address the concern, with other offenses perceived as more important or relevant. According to feminism, if law enforcement took the act of sexual assault more seriously, financing would be available at all levels (e.g., university police departments, hospitals, crime laboratories) to ensure the timely processing of SAKs; accordingly, female victims of sexual assault crimes would find their cases perceived with importance and equity.

## Theme 2 Discussion: Resources

RDT indicates that organizational growth requires the maximization of resources through mergers, alliances, and collaboration (Taylor et al., 2018). The findings from the study indicated the relevance of RDT specific to SAK processing by university police officers. Participants overwhelmingly identified limited resources as a barrier to processing SAKs. Consistent with the theory, officers reported having directly and indirectly requesting additional resources for timely processing of SAKs, valid results, apprehension of the perpetrator, and victim support beyond the traumatic experience, all of which is consistent with the current research surrounding SAK processing (Garza & Franklin, 2020; Lovell, Huang, et al., 2020). In short, the officers noted the need for resources to address the problem of unsubmitted and untested SAKs.

Functionalism indicates that all aspects of a society serve a purpose and are necessary for long-term survival (Laluddin, 2016). The purpose of the police department is to provide law and order so that people can function within a safe environment. The extremely high number of sexual assault crimes against women (CDC, 2015) means that (a) the system designed to provide law and order is not functioning properly, (b) the system designed to serve and protect does not adequately serve and protect female survivors of sexual assault, or (c) the system is functioning as designed. Regardless of which proposal one accepts, the continual distribution of resources promotes the dysfunction that often leaves female survivors of sexual assault without proper closure.

Feminism shows the important role women of women in society (Tripathi, 2014), yet acknowledges that women face ongoing oppression, domination, powerlessness, and inequality with male counterparts (Turner & Maschi, 2015). University police officers acknowledged the problem of female victimization by sexual assault and the related problems of untested and unsubmitted SAKs. However, participants also noted that, although resources might be available to address other criminal matters, funds to address unsubmitted and untested SAKs are minimal. Under a feminist lens, resource allocation decisions that fail to support female victims by ensuring the processing of SAKs are a continuation of the oppression and domination that promote powerlessness and inequality for women. The limited resources that serve as a barrier to processing SAKs indicate that the concern is not important enough to adequately fund. Alternately, or in addition, it seems that law enforcement does not value women and the issues they face, despite the detrimental, generational impact of sexual abuse on individuals.

## Theme 3 Discussion: Manpower

RDT also conveys that by working together, individuals within the organization gain the motivation and trust to develop and expand coalitions (Spohn & Tellis, 2019; Taylor et al., 2018). The findings from the study support the relevance of the theory in examining university law enforcement officials and SAKs. Officers in the study noted a lack of human resources, which negatively impacted the investigation and processing of SAKs. Because of the limited number of officers, law enforcement organizations are unable to assign working teams to address SAK processing; similarly, agencies cannot hire sufficient staff to work in the crime labs or expand current services related to SAK submission and testing.

Applicable to the study, functionalism indicates that police officers operate within a society with legitimate rights, including arresting members of society who do not obey the laws (Lawson, 2014). Due to limited manpower within the university setting, police officers focus on other legal matters, having minimal roles in addressing sexual assault and processing SAKs. After officers take statements from victims and transport them to the hospital, they transfer the case to the local police department. In summary and consistent with the literature, the officers suggested that increased manpower could help them fulfill the responsibilities associated with addressing the unsubmitted, untested SAKs (cf. Crouse et al., 2019; Hendrix et al., 2019).

Also in line with feminist theory is that society should view women as equal to men; accordingly, women should object to having an unequal position in society (Hirudayaraj & Shields, 2019). Of interest is that the majority of police officers are men, including those who handle sexual assault cases, whereas most of the reported sexual assault victims are female. Accordingly, female victims, including those experiencing the trauma of sexual assault by a male perpetrator, are dependent upon a male-dominated system to ensure the investigation and fair processing of their cases. According to feminist theory, the backlog of untested and unsubmitted SAKs is an indication that the male-dominated profession may be insensitive to or uncommitted to resolving the issue that primarily impacts women. Addressing manpower needs by hiring additional female officers and placing them in positions to influence the investigation and processing of sexual assault could help to reduce the backlog of SAK submission and testing.

## Theme 4 Discussion: Reoccurrence

RDT highlights the significance of collaboration and interagency dependence based on trust and motivation to acquire and provide resources. In relation to the theory, university police officers overwhelmingly noted that perpetrators will continue to reoffend, particularly if not held accountable for the sexual assault crimes they have committed. Unfortunately, the backlog of SAKs facilitates reoffense. Participants also reported collaborating with other medical facilities and police departments to address sexual assault crimes; however, the numbers of unsubmitted and untested SAKs remain high, possibly as a result of limitations related to manpower, resources, and finances. Perhaps increased collaborative efforts aimed at improving the acquisition and provision of resources, manpower, and finances could improve SAK processing, leading to the arrests of perpetrators and curtailing reoccurrence. The consideration is consistent with the literature on officers' direct and indirect requests for additional, collaborative resources to process SAKs. More timely processing would lead to apprehending perpetrators and removing them from the streets, thus minimizing their ability to reoffend (Lovell, Huang, et al., 2020; National Institute of Justice, 2015; Quinlan, 2020).

Functionalism pertains to the socialization of members within groups and organizations, such as those operating in law enforcement, to demonstrate consensus in supporting the norms and guidelines within the group or organization (Lawson, 2014). Significant numbers of sexual assaults and reoffending perpetrators indicate that not all members of the group are functioning consistently within the established structure and guidelines for processing SAKs. Although functionalism was not a specified theme, participants had little knowledge regarding procedures and policies related to SAKs after they transferred the case. The limited information could partially explain the inconsistent application of present policies that, if consistently used by all individuals within the policing organization, should lead to higher arrest rates for sexual assault perpetrators and less reoccurrence of sexual assaults by serial perpetrators.

Feminist theory indicates that feminism is not one ideology but consists of a range of political and social movements focused on fighting and promoting gender equality (Turner & Maschi, 2015). The backlog of unsubmitted and untested SAKs and the high rate of reoccurrence by perpetrators should be of heightened interest for those concerned with gender equality as espoused by feminist theory. Because the majority of victims reporting sexual assault crimes are women, feminist theory is an appropriate foundation to argue for increased political and social movements focused on fighting against sex crimes. Present-day feminism is consistent with the women's movements of the past (Quinlan, 2020; Whalley, 2020).

In summary, the findings of the qualitative research align with the literature on the subject of unsubmitted, untested SAKs. Officials within the law enforcement community could use the findings to initiate a sophisticated evaluation. The findings indicated the possibility of utilizing the necessary resources.

## Conclusions Based on the Results

The study's findings aligned with the existing literature on unsubmitted and untested SAKs. Despite the limitations, the research showed that adequate finances, resources, and manpower could minimize the problems related to unsubmitted and untested SAKs, including reoccurrence by perpetrators. Ultimately, the considerations will require collaborative approaches, increased hiring of female officers, and greater knowledge regarding SAK processing to reduce sexual assault crimes and the number of unsubmitted and untested SAKs.

## Comparison of Findings with Theoretical Framework and Previous Literature

The findings in the study had a strong connection with the three underlying theories. Each of the theories provided a framework for understanding, interpreting, and presenting the findings. In line with feminist theory, sexual assault is a significant issue that impacts women and needs additional advocacy. The majority of victims of sexual assault are females; however, there are minimal processes and procedures for protecting and advocating for women, leaving them powerless in many ways. The high number of unsubmitted and untested SAKs, coupled with the limited resources, finances, and manpower available for addressing the issue, aligns with aspects of feminist theory, including gender, power, and oppression. Further illustration of feminist theory also comes from the low percentage of women available for the study.

Functionalism presents sexual assault in the university setting as an issue that receives little focus. The role is minimal pertaining to sexual assault. Limited budgets impact officers' ability to protect victims, thus failing to hold perpetrators accountable. The current distribution of resources promotes dysfunction, with little to no closure for the victim due to high rates of unprosecuted offenders and crime reoccurrence. Participants' responses aligned with aspects of functionalism, including collective, social order, and conscience.

Finally, RDT had a strong presence in the findings. Law enforcement officers affirmed the relevance of RDT when they noted their minimal involvement in SAK processing. Due to limited resources, the officers had few, if any, roles in processing SAKs. In addition, although the literature showed that officers have received trauma impact training, none of the participants reported having any training on issues such as sexual assault. The officers noted the need for a collective emphasis on addressing sexual assault and SAKs, and the recognition that the emphasis must come from a variety of stakeholders, including officials from the mayor's office and community agencies. The responses show the aspects of RDT, such as resource limitations and collective responsibility.

These findings within the theme align with the literature showing that limited finances, including funding for testing, have an impact on SAK processing (Campbell, Fehler-Cabral, Bybee, et al., 2017; Crouse et al., 2019; Hendrix et al., 2019). The participants' responses indicated the impact of insufficient funds on the continuation of sexual assaults. Agencies do not have the finances, resources, or manpower to process the kits.

The participants' responses indicated that limited resources are a barrier when processing SAKs and that the limitation has further impacts. The findings within the theme align with the literature showing that limited resources for testing have an impact on SAK processing (Campbell, Fehler-Cabral, Bybee, et al., 2017; Crouse et al., 2019; Hendrix et al., 2019). Although some blame the police for not storing, submitting, and successfully tracking SAK evidence, others find fault with crime labs, where excessive workload and limited resources obstruct the ability to process and test kits within a reasonable timeframe (Campbell & Fehler-Cabral, 2016; Pinchevsky, 2016). In addition, investigators and prosecutors do not believe that using funding for test kits for victims who might not take their cases to court is a good use of already-limited resources (Campbell, Fehler-Cabral, Bybee, et al.; Maguire et al., 2015).

These findings align with the literature showing that personnel issues, including staffing cuts, can have a long-term, negative impact on sexual assault investigations (Campbell, Fehler-Cabral, Bybee, et al., 2017). In addition, limited manpower has had an effect on conducting investigations and providing support to the victims. Consequently, most crime labs are not able to process the kits.

These findings align with the literature showing that offenders can commit subsequent crimes because they have not been apprehended. The common practice of not submitting or testing SAKs could reasonably lead to the perpetration of additional sexual assaults by the same offender (Carvalho et al., 2020). Participants also acknowledged that accountability depended on identifying and arresting the perpetrator (cf. Lovell et al., 2018). The backlog of SAK submissions and testing indicates barriers and gaps that result in the potential for continued sexual assaults by the perpetrators (Lovell et al., 2020). Thus, when using DNA analysis, the perpetrator can be prosecuted, vindicating those who have been wrongly accused and revealing repeat offenders (Campbell et al., 2020). Furthermore, the findings show that sexual assault has a significant impact on the emotional well-being of victims who may choose to discontinue interacting with law enforcement due to the requirement of reliving the traumatic experience (Garza & Franklin, 2020), which is a perceived barrier. Finally, the findings show that the barriers and gaps in processing kits create the potential for continued sexual assaults by the perpetrators (Lovell, Huang, et al., 2020).

## Interpretation of the Findings

After the themes arose from the data analysis, it was essential to establish whether they were sufficient to answer the research questions. The following section contains a clarification of the themes in line with the research questions to assess the study's findings. The third research question was related to barriers that could cause delayed processing of SAKs. In response to the question, three themes emerged: finances, resources, and manpower. Overwhelmingly, participants indicated that departments do not have the finances, resources, and manpower to process the large volume of SAKs, with resources cited as an overwhelming concern. The findings in the study align with other research that shows the problem of insufficient resources for addressing the kit backlog (Hendrix et al., 2019). Moreover, there is a need for more resources to help departments process unsubmitted, untested SAKs. Perhaps the themes are why there have been no new developments for SAK processing.

The fifth research question was about the impact the backlog has on offender accountability. In response to the question, the theme "reoccurrence" emerged. The participants offered that unless the perpetrators are arrested, they will continue to commit sexual assaults. The findings in the study align with other research showing that perpetrators will reoffend until apprehended (Lovell, Huang, et al., 2020). Therefore, there is a need for more manpower to get the perpetrators into police custody so they cannot continue to commit sexual assault, thus reducing the number of SAKs for processing.

In summary, the findings of the qualitative research align with the prior literature on the subject of unsubmitted, untested SAKs. Officials within the law enforcement community could use the findings as the beginning of the conversation for a sophisticated level of logical evaluation. The findings indicated the possibility for the implementation of resources.

## Limitations

As with all research, there were limitations in the study, the first being the collection of data through individual interviews. Personal interviews posed a limitation because the self-reported responses presented the attitudes and beliefs of university law enforcement officials at one point in time versus over a period. A second limitation was the recruitment strategy. As permission was sought for community or campus police departments to participate in the study, recruitment was a challenge due to the unwillingness of law enforcement administrators to officially and publicly discuss the issue of unsubmitted, untested SAKs. Recruiting participants was an enormous challenge. In addition, the perceived factors impacting the submission and processing of SAKs at two university campuses was focused on instead of at a large, metropolitan police department. Unsuccessful attempts were made to include officers from larger departments; as such, the current study had a narrower focus and fewer participants from two small university police departments.

Additionally, due to the small sample size and minimal geographic, racial, and gender diversity, the results may not be generalizable to other university or college campuses or geographic areas. A final limitation surrounds the alignment between interview and research questions. Some of the interview questions specific to Research Questions 1, 2, and 4 needed reframing, with prompts utilized to garner more direct answers to those questions.

## Implications of the Study

There are millions of women world-wide who are impacted by this phenomenon; thus, their daughters will be impacted also for years to come. The findings inspire a needed conversation within U.S. police departments regarding how to solve the problem of unsubmitted and untested SAKs so that sexual assault victims can achieve justice. More financial resources need to be allotted to develop a database for tracking and prioritizing SAKs. A training program needs to be developed for individuals who work with the victims of sexual assault. The study provides a unique context to academic literature in the criminal justice field. Through the lens of several theories, including RDT (Percy et al., 2015), the study helps to advance the scientific knowledge base of SAKs and the perceptions of university police officers. For example, RDT could guide further policy considerations about sexual assault and the development of university campus provisions.

The results might also influence the law enforcement community by providing an understanding and rationale as to why SAKs remain untested. Policymakers and law enforcement officers could draw upon the research in changing policies and procedures when assisting victims of sexual assault, as well as when developing training resources for police officers. Furthermore, the research could influence hospital policies and procedures of SANEs when they conduct invasive examinations on victims of sexual assault.

Additionally, the findings show the need for improvement in timely response to sexual assault. The necessity of processing kits promptly has implications for the victims, perpetrators, and society. In addition, when law enforcement fails to respond swiftly, the perpetrator remains free and could commit additional crimes.

Ideally, there is no one way to tackle this phenomenon but with collaboration of the various stakeholders (law enforcement, prosecutors, medical professionals, and forensic laboratories) transformation can be created with combined resources and levels of expertise.

## Recommendations for Further Research

Recommendations of the current research study inform future researchers wanting to conduct the study. The foundation has been positioned for future considerations. Future studies are necessary so researchers are able to conduct the research on a greater level to gain a deeper understanding of the phenomenon of unsubmitted and untested sexual assault kits. The subsequent dialogue comprises recommendations developed directly from the data, recommendations derived from methodological, research design, or other limitations, recommendations based on delimitations and recommendations to investigate issues not supported by the data but relevant to the research problem.

### Recommendations Developed Directly from the Data

The findings of the study answered two of the research questions therefore prompting areas of future research. One suggestion is the inclusion of focus groups, which would allow law enforcement officials to hear officers' responses and discussions and collectively develop strategies to resolve the issue of unsubmitted and untested SAKs. Another recommendation is for researchers to repeat the study in other areas of the United States. Related to the replication of the study is the suggestion to add a quantitative component. Scholars could use the recommendations to validate or even challenge the results of the study, as a survey instrument with numbers and Likert-scale ratings could provide a measurable, accurate response. A future researcher could adopt a quantitative approach with surveys or questionnaires (Franklin et al., 2020).

## Recommendations Derived from Methodological, Research Design, or Other Limitations

One suggestion is the inclusion of focus groups, which would allow law enforcement officials to hear officers' responses and discussions and collectively develop strategies to resolve the issue of unsubmitted and untested SAKs. Another recommendation is for researchers to repeat the study in other areas of the United States. Related to the replication of the study is the suggestion to add a quantitative component. Scholars could use the recommendations to validate or even challenge the results of the study, as a survey instrument with numbers and Likert-scale ratings could provide a measurable, accurate response. A future researcher could adopt a quantitative approach with surveys or questionnaires.

Participants in the study were officers from two university law enforcement agencies. A limitation of the study was that the researcher did not conduct the study at major metropolitan agencies or agencies across the United States. Numerous cities and states have announced additional resources to process untested SAKs (Campbell & Fehler-Cabral, 2020). Hence, a quantitative approach with data collected from various states would provide valuable measurements for law enforcement officials and policymakers to draw upon in making better decisions regarding resources for unsubmitted, untested SAKs.

From law enforcement and criminal justice perspectives, police officers, lawyers, judges, and crime lab technicians should be able to rethink the use and value of SAKs for cases, in addition to improving the process for SAK collection and submission. If members of all parties realized that every decision, they make has an impact on another level within the criminal justice system, they could likely correct the backlog. At present, the decisions made about SAK submission and testing still cause delays and might even result in lost or mishandled kits. On a national level, any attempts to reduce backlogged kits should include a plan to develop a more efficient inventory system; implementation should incorporate standard procedures for local, state, and federal levels.

Future researchers could use a broader demographic population and more diverse law enforcement agencies, whereas the only agencies in the study were university law enforcement agencies. By conducting quantitative research, researchers could collect and analyze additional data on unsubmitted and untested SAKs.

## Recommendations Based on Delimitations

Future research studies should be limited to posing interview questions that align and answer the research question. Finally, future researchers should obtain the input of law enforcement officers of other races.

## Recommendations to Investigate Issues Not Supported by the Data, But Relevant to the Research Problem

Future researchers should clarify the definition of *resources*. In the study, law enforcement officials referred to finances, resources, and manpower, all of which are types of resources. Scholars could interpret the theme "resources" as incorporating both finances and manpower. The issue of the influence of gender was an issue that was not supported by the data but were relevant to the research problem.

## Conclusion

The purpose of the research study was to explore university law enforcement officials' perceptions regarding unsubmitted, untested SAKs. Stakeholders, such as members of law enforcement agencies, prosecutors, victims' services, medical professionals, and forensic laboratories, could benefit from the study's findings and recommendations regarding finances, resources, manpower, and reoccurrence.

University law enforcement officers are generally the first to respond to reports of sexual assault crimes on college and university campuses. As first responders, officers are responsible for handling sexual assault accusations consistently. The research shows that the provision of resources, finances, and manpower is necessary to reduce single and reoccurring sexual assault crimes, and to promote the proper functions of the criminal justice system, collective engagement of members of society, and equal value of citizens, regardless of gender. The study showed the need for stakeholders to collectively engage, acknowledge the systemic gaps, and provide resolution so that officials properly utilize SAKs to apprehend offenders and empower victims to live healthy and functional lives.

# BIBLIOGRAPHY

Agarin, Timofey. "5 Functionalism and Its Legacy." In *The SAGE Handbook of Political Science,* 83-95. London: SAGE Publications, 2020.

Amankwaa, Aaron Opoku, and Carole McCartney. "The Effectiveness of the UK National DNA Database." *Forensic Science International: Synergy* 1 (2019): 45-55.

Anasti, Theresa. "'Officers Are Doing the Best They Can': Concerns Around Law Enforcement and Social Service Collaboration in Service Provision to Sex Workers." *Affilia* 35, no. 1 (2020): 49-72.

Beaudry, Jeffrey S., and Lynne Miller. *Research Literacy: A Primer for Understanding and Using Research.* New York: Guilford Press, 2016.

Beauregard, Eric, and Melissa Martineau. "No Body, No Crime? The Role of Forensic Awareness in Avoiding Police Detection in Cases of Sexual Homicide." *Journal of Criminal Justice* 42, no. 2 (2014): 213-220.

Bee, Beth A. "Power, Perception, and Adaptation: Exploring Gender and Social–Environmental Risk Perception in Northern Guanajuato, Mexico." *Geoforum* 69 (2016): 71-80.

Beitin, Ben K. "Interview and Sampling: How Many and Whom." In *The SAGE handbook of interview research: The complexity of the craft,* 243-254. Thousand Oaks: SAGE Publications, 2012.

Biana, Hazel Tionloc. "Extending bell hooks' Feminist Theory." *Journal of International Women's Studies* 21, no. 1 (2020): 13-29.

Brinkmann, Svend, and Steinar Kvale. "Ethics in qualitative psychological research." In *The SAGE Handbook of Qualitative Research in Psychology,* 263-279. Thousand Oaks, CA: SAGE Publications, 2017.

Burke, Tarana. "The Inception." Last modified 2013. http://justbeinc.wixsite.com/justbeinc/the-me-too-movement-cmml

Caelli, Kate, Lynne Ray, and Judy Mill. "'Clear as Mud': Toward Greater Clarity in Generic Qualitative Research." *International Journal of Qualitative Methods* 2, no. 2 (2003): 1-13.

Campbell, Rebecca, and Giannina Fehler-Cabral. "Accountability, Collaboration, and Social Change: Ethical Tensions in an Action Research Project to Address Untested Sexual Assault Kits (SAKs)." *American Journal of Community Psychology* 60, no. 3-4 (2017): 476-482.

—. "The Best Way Out Is Always Through: Addressing the Problem of Untested Sexual Assault Kits (SAKs) Through Multidisciplinary Collaboration." *Victims & Offenders* 15, no. 2 (2020): 159-173.

—. "Why Police 'Couldn't or Wouldn't' Submit Sexual Assault Kits for Forensic DNA Testing: A Focal Concerns Theory Analysis of Untested Rape Kits." *Law & Society Review* 52, no. 1 (2018): 73-105.

Campbell, Rebecca, Giannina Fehler-Cabral, and Sheena Horsford. "Creating a Victim Notification Protocol for Untested Sexual Assault Kits: An Empirically Supported Planning Framework." *Journal of Forensic Nursing* 13, no. 1 (2017): 3-13.

Campbell, Rebecca, Giannina Fehler-Cabral, Deborah Bybee, and Jessica Shaw. "Forgotten Evidence: A Mixed Methods Study of Why Sexual Assault Kits (SAKs) Are Not Submitted for DNA Forensic Testing." *Law and Human Behavior* 41, no. 5 (2017): 454.

Campbell, Rebecca, Hannah Feeney, Giannina Fehler-Cabral, Jessica Shaw, and Sheena Horsford. "The National Problem of Untested Sexual Assault Kits (SAKs): Scope, Causes, and Future Directions for Research, Policy, and Practice." *Trauma, Violence, & Abuse* 18, no. 4 (2017): 363-376.

Campbell, Rebecca, Hannah Feeney, Rachael Goodman-Williams, Dhruv B. Sharma, and Steven J. Pierce. "Connecting the Dots: Identifying Suspected Serial Sexual Offenders Through Forensic DNA Evidence." *Psychology of Violence* 10, no. 3 (2020): 255.

Campbell, Rebecca, Jessica Shaw, and Giannina Fehler-Cabral. "Evaluation of a Victim-Centered, Trauma-Informed Victim Notification Protocol for Untested Sexual Assault Kits (SAKs)." *Violence Against Women* 24, no. 4 (2018): 379-400.

Campbell, Rebecca, Jessica Shaw, and Giannina Fehler-Cabral. "Shelving Justice: The Discovery of Thousands of Untested Rape Kits in Detroit." *City & Community* 14, no. 2 (2015): 151-166.

Campbell, Rebecca, Steven J. Pierce, Dhruv B. Sharma, Hannah Feeney, and Giannina Fehler-Cabral. "Should rape kit testing be prioritized by victim–offender relationship? Empirical comparison of forensic testing outcomes for stranger and nonstranger sexual assaults." *Criminology & Public Policy* 15, no. 2 (2016): 555-583.

Campbell, Rebecca, Steven J. Pierce, Dhruv B. Sharma, Hannah Feeney, and Giannina Fehler-Cabral. "Developing empirically informed policies for sexual assault kit DNA testing: is it too late to test kits beyond the statute of limitations?" *Criminal Justice Policy Review* 30, no. 1 (2019): 3-27.

Campbell, Rebecca, Steven J. Pierce, Wenjuan Ma, Hannah Feeney, Rachael Goodman-Williams, and Dhruv B. Sharma. "Will History Repeat Itself? Growth Mixture Modeling of Suspected Serial Sexual Offending Using Forensic DNA Evidence." *Journal of Criminal Justice* 61 (2019): 1-12.

Carvalho, Nígela Rodrigues, Grasielly de Oliveira Lázaro Arão, Yanna Andressa Ramos Lima, Neide Maria de Oliveira Godinho, Mariana Flavia Mota, and Thaís Cidália Vieira Gigonzag. "The Contribution of DNA Databases for Stored Sexual Crimes Evidences in the Central of Brazil." *Forensic Science International: Genetics* 46 (2020): 102235.

Centers for Disease Control and Prevention. 2015. "National Intimate Partner and Sexual Violence Survey." https://www.cdc.gov/violenceprevention/datasources/nisvs/index.html

—. 2018. "Sexual Violence Is Preventable." Accessed June 16, 2021. https://www.cdc.gov/injury/features/sexual-violence/index.html

Chang, Yen-Ping, and Sara B. Algoe. "On Thanksgiving: Cultural Variation in Gratitude Demonstrations and Perceptions Between the United States and Taiwan." *Emotion* 20, no. 7 (2019): 1185-1205.

Chrisley, Ron, and Aaron Sloman. "Functionalism, Revisionism, and Qualia." *APA Newsletter on Philosophy and Computers* 16, no. 1 (2016): 2-13.

Clark, Michelle, James Gill, Kristin Sasinouski, and Angela McGuire. "Cold Case Homicides: DNA Testing of Retained Autopsy Sexual Assault Smears." *Journal of Forensic Sciences* 64, no. 4 (2019): 1100-1104.

Connelly, F. Michael, and D. Jean Clandinin. "Stories of Experience and Narrative Inquiry." *Educational Researcher* 19, no. 5 (1990): 2-14.

Creswell, John W. *Mapping the Field of Mixed Methods Research.* Thousand Oaks, CA: SAGE Publications, 2009.

—. *Qualitative Inquiry & Research Design: Choosing Among Five Approaches* (3rd ed.). Thousand Oaks, CA: SAGE Publications, 2013.

—. *Research Design: Qualitative, Quantitative, and Mixed Methods Approaches*. Thousand Oaks, CA: SAGE Publications, 2014, Kindle.

Cross, Theodore P., and Thaddeus Schmitt. "Forensic Medical Results and Law Enforcement Actions Following Sexual Assault: A Comparison of Child, Adolescent and Adult Cases." *Child Abuse & Neglect* 93 (2019): 103-110.

Crouse, Cecelia A., Lawrence Bauer, Tara Sessa, Amelia Looper, Julie Sikorsky, and Dustin T. Yeatman. "Combined DNA Index System (CODIS)-Based Analysis of Untested Sexual Assault Evidence in Palm Beach County Florida." *Forensic Science International: Synergy* 1 (2019): 253-270.

Daly, Anya. "A Phenomenological Grounding of Feminist Ethics." *Journal of the British Society for Phenomenology* 50, no. 1 (2019): 1-18.

Davis, Robert C., Bernard Auchter, William Wells, Torie Camp, and Susan Howley. "The Effects of Legislation Mandating DNA Testing in Sexual Assault Cases: Results in Texas." *Violence Against Women* 26, no. 5 (2020): 417-437.

Davis, Robert C., and William Wells. "DNA Testing in Sexual Assault Cases: When Do the Benefits Outweigh the Costs?" *Forensic Science International* 299 (2019): 44-48.

Deslatte, Aaron, and Eric Stokan. "Hierarchies of Need in Sustainable Development: A Resource Dependence Approach for Local Governance." *Urban Affairs Review* 55, no. 4 (2019): 1125-1152.

Dixon, Carmen S. "Interviewing Adolescent Females in Qualitative Research." *Qualitative Report* 20, no. 12 (2015).

Duriesmith, David. "Friends Don't Let Friends Cite the Malestream: A Case for Strategic Silence in Feminist International Relations." *International Feminist Journal of Politics* 22, no. 1 (2020): 26-32.

Fallik, Seth W., Ross Deuchar, Vaughn J. Crichlow, and Hannah Hodges. "Policing Through Social Media: A Qualitative Exploration." *International Journal of Police Science & Management* 22, no. 2 (2020): 208-218.

Fallik, Seth W., and William Wells. "Testing Previously Unsubmitted Sexual Assault Kits: What Are the Investigative Results?" *Criminal Justice Policy Review* 26, no. 6 (2015): 598-619.

Federal Bureau of Investigation. 2014. "Crime in the U.S." https://ucr.fbi.gov/crime-in-the-u.s

Feeney, Hannah, Rebecca Campbell, and Debi Cain. "Do You Wish to Prosecute the Person Who Assaulted You? Untested Sexual Assault Kits and Victim Notification of Rape Survivors Assaulted as Adolescents." *Victims & Offenders* 13, no. 5 (2018): 651-674.

Ferguson, Christopher J., and Richard D. Hartley. "The Pleasure Is Momentary… The Expense Damnable? The Influence of Pornography on Rape and Sexual Assault." *Aggression and Violent Behavior* 14, no. 5 (2009): 323-329.

Fisher, William A., Taylor Kohut, Lisha A. Di Gioacchino, and Paul Fedoroff. "Pornography, Sex Crime, and Paraphilia." *Current Psychiatry Reports* 15, no. 6 (2013): 362.

Fletcher, Luke. "How Can Personal Development Lead to Increased Engagement? The Roles of Meaningfulness and Perceived Line Manager Relations." *The International Journal of Human Resource Management* 30, no. 7 (2019): 1203-1226.

Foubert, John D., Angela Clark-Taylor, and Andrew F. Wall. "Is Campus Rape Primarily a Serial or One-Time Problem? Evidence from a Multicampus Study." *Violence Against Women* 26, no. 3-4 (2020): 296-311.

Franklin, Cortney A., Alondra D. Garza, Amanda Goodson, and Leana Allen Bouffard. "Police Perceptions of Crime Victim Behaviors: A Trend Analysis Exploring Mandatory Training and Knowledge of Sexual and Domestic Violence Survivors' Trauma Responses." *Crime & Delinquency* 66, no. 8 (2020): 1055-1086.

Garza, Alondra D., and Cortney A. Franklin. "The Effect of Rape Myth Endorsement on Police Response to Sexual Assault Survivors." *Violence Against Women* 27, no. 3-4 (2021): 552-573.

Giblin, Matthew J., and George W. Burruss. "Developing a Measurement Model of Institutional Processes in Policing." *Policing: An International Journal of Police Strategies & Management* 32, no. 2: 351-376 (2009).

Giorgi, Amedeo P., and Barbro M. Giorgi. "The Descriptive Phenomenological Psychological Method." *Phenomenological Psychology* 43, no. 1: 3-12 (2003).

Glaser, Barney G. *Theoretical Sensitivity: Advances in the Methodology of Grounded Theory*. Mill Valley, CA: Sociology Press, 1978.

Goldman, Rachael. "When Is Due Process Due? The Impact of Title IX Sexual Assault Adjudication on the Rights of University Students." *Pepperdine Law Review* 47 (2019): 185.

Goodman-Williams, Rachael, Rebecca Campbell, Dhruv B. Sharma, Steven J. Pierce, Hannah Feeney, and Giannina Fehler-Cabral. "How to Right a Wrong: Empirically Evaluating Whether Victim, Offender, and Assault Characteristics Can Inform Rape Kit Testing Policies." *Journal of Trauma & Dissociation* 20, no. 3 (2019): 288-303.

Grey, Daniel. "'Monstrous and indefensible'? Newspaper accounts of sexual assaults on children in nineteenth-century England and Wales." In *Women's Criminality in Europe, 1600–1914*, 189-205. London: Cambridge University Press, 2020.

Gyurák Babel'ová, Zdenka, Augustín Stareček, Kristína Koltnerová, and Dagmar Cagáňová. "Perceived Organizational Performance in Recruiting and Retaining Employees with Respect to Different Generational Groups of Employees and Sustainable Human Resource Management." *Sustainability* 12, no. 2 (2020): 574.

Hald, Gert Martin, Neil M. Malamuth, and Carlin Yuen. "Pornography and Attitudes Supporting Violence Against Women: Revisiting the Relationship in Nonexperimental Studies." *Aggressive Behavior: Official Journal of the International Society for Research on Aggression* 36, no. 1 (2010): 14-20.

Harris, Andrew J., Karen J. Terry, and Alissa R. Ackerman. "Campus Sexual Assault: Forging an Action-Focused Research Agenda." *Sexual Abuse* 31, no. 3 (2019): 263-269.

Haskell, Lori, and Melanie Randall. "Impact of trauma on adult sexual assault victims: What the criminal justice system needs to know." *Available at SSRN 3417763* (2019).

Hendrix, Joshua A., Kevin J. Strom, William J. Parish, Patricia A. Melton, and Amanda Royal Young. "An Examination of Sexual Assault Kit Submission Efficiencies Among a Nationally Representative Sample of Law Enforcement Agencies." *Criminal Justice Policy Review* 31, no. 7 (2020): 1095-1115.

Hill, Amber L., Elizabeth Miller, Kelley A. Jones, Robert WS Coulter, Kaleab Abebe, Heather McCauley, Dana L. Rofey et al. "Intimate Partner Violence Victimization Histories and their Association with Alcohol Use Patterns Among College Students." *Journal of Adolescent Health* 66, no. 2 (2020): S34.

Hine, Benjamin, and Anthony Murphy. "The Influence of 'High' vs. 'Low' Rape Myth Acceptance on Police Officers' Judgements of Victim and Perpetrator Responsibility, and Rape Authenticity." *Journal of Criminal Justice* 60 (2019): 100-107.

Hirudayaraj, Malar, and Lauren Shields. "Feminist Theory: A Research Agenda for HRD." *Advances in Developing Human Resources* 21, no. 3 (2019): 319-334.

Holland, Kathryn J., Amber M. Gustafson, Lilia M. Cortina, and Allison E. Cipriano. "Supporting Survivors: The Roles of Rape Myths and Feminism in University Resident Assistants' Response to Sexual Assault Disclosure Scenarios." *Sex Roles* 82, no. 3 (2020): 206-218.

Huq, Afreen, Caroline Swee Lin Tan, and Vidhula Venugopal. "How Do Women Entrepreneurs Strategize Growth? An Investigation Using the Social Feminist Theory Lens." *Journal of Small Business Management* 58, no. 2 (2020): 259-287.

Inciarte, A., L. Leal, L. Masfarre, E. Gonzalez, V. Diaz-Brito, C. Lucero, J. Garcia-Pindado et al. "Post-Exposure Prophylaxis for HIV Infection in Sexual Assault Victims." *HIV Medicine* 21, no. 1 (2020): 43-52.

Jakobsen, Siri. "Managing Tension in Coopetition Through Mutual Dependence and Asymmetries: A Longitudinal Study of a Norwegian R&D Alliance." *Industrial Marketing Management* 84 (2020): 251-260.

Kahlke, Renate M. "Generic Qualitative Approaches: Pitfalls and Benefits of Methodological Mixology." *International Journal of Qualitative Methods* 13, no. 1 (2014): 37-52.

Kalu, Kalu N. "Institution-Building, Not Nation-Building: A Structural-Functional Model." *International Review of Administrative Sciences* 77, no. 1 (2011): 119-137.

Kerka, Jaimie E., Derek J. Heckman, James H. Albert, Jon E. Sprague, and Lewis O. Maddox. "Statistical Modeling of the Case Information from the Ohio Attorney General's Sexual Assault Kit Testing Initiative." *Journal of Forensic Sciences* 63, no. 4 (2018): 1122-1133.

Kettrey, Heather Hensman, and Robert A. Marx. "Does the Gendered Approach of Bystander Programs Matter in the Prevention of Sexual Assault Among Adolescents and College Students? A Systematic Review and Meta-Analysis." *Archives of Sexual Behavior* 48, no. 7 (2019): 2037-2053.

Khan, Shamus, Joss Greene, Claude Ann Mellins, and Jennifer S. Hirsch. "The Social Organization of Sexual Assault." *Annual Review of Criminology* 3 (2020): 139-163.

Kirk-Provencher, Katelyn T., Melissa R. Schick, Nichea S. Spillane, and Allison Tobar-Santamaria. "History of Sexual Assault, Past-Year Alcohol Use, and Alcohol-Related Problems in American Indian Adolescents." *Addictive Behaviors* 108 (2020): 106441.

Kiyimba, Nikki, and Michelle O'Reilly. "The Risk of Secondary Traumatic Stress in the Qualitative Transcription Process: A Research Note." *Qualitative Research* 16, no. 4 (2016): 468-476.

Knapp, Joshua R., Marjo-Riitta Diehl, and William Dougan. "Towards a Social-Cognitive Theory of Multiple Psychological Contracts." *European Journal of Work and Organizational Psychology* 29, no. 2 (2020): 200-214.

Laluddin, Hayatullah. "A Review of Three Major Sociological Theories and an Islamic Perspective." *International Journal of Islamic Thought* 10 (2016): 8.

Lang, Heather. "# MeToo: A Case Study in Re-Embodying Information." *Computers and Composition* 53 (2019): 9-20.

Lathan, Emma, Jennifer Langhinrichsen-Rohling, Jessica Duncan, and James Tres Stefurak. "The Promise Initiative: Promoting a Trauma-Informed Police Response to Sexual Assault in a Mid-Size Southern Community." *Journal of Community Psychology* 47, no. 7 (2019): 1733-1749.

Lawson, Celeste. "Situating Policing in a Late Modern Society: The Ontology of Police Identity." *The Police Journal* 87, no. 4 (2014): 270-276.

Leedy, Paul D. and Jeanne Ellis Ormrod. *Practical Research Design Planning and Design* (10th ed.). Upper Saddle River, NJ: Pearson Education, 2010.

Lovell, Rachel, Misty Luminais, Daniel J. Flannery, Richard Bell, and Brett Kyker. "Describing the Process and Quantifying the Outcomes of the Cuyahoga County Sexual Assault Kit Initiative." *Journal of Criminal Justice* 57 (2018): 106-115.

Lovell, Rachel, Wenxuan Huang, Laura Overman, Daniel Flannery, and Joanna Klingenstein. "Offending Histories and Typologies of Suspected Sexual Offenders Identified via Untested Sexual Assault Kits." *Criminal Justice and Behavior* 47, no. 4 (2020): 470-486.

Maguire, Edward R., William R. King, William Wells, and Charles M. Katz. "Potential Unintended Consequences of the Movement Toward Forensic Laboratory Independence." *Police Quarterly* 18, no. 3 (2015): 272-292.

Malterud, Kirsti, Volkert Dirk Siersma, and Ann Dorrit Guassora. "Sample Size in Qualitative Interview Studies: Guided by Information Power." *Qualitative Health Research* 26, no. 13 (2016): 1753-1760.

McAndrew, William P., and Max M. Houck. "Interpol Review of Forensic Science Management Literature 2016–2019." *Forensic Science International: Synergy* 3 (2020): 382-388.

Menaker, Tasha A., Bradley A. Campbell, and William Wells. "The Use of Forensic Evidence in Sexual Assault Investigations: Perceptions of Sex Crimes Investigators." *Violence Against Women* 23, no. 4 (2017): 399-425.

Merriam, Sharan B. *Qualitative Research: A Guide to Design and Implementation*. San Francisco: Jossey-Bass, 2009.

—. *Qualitative Research: A Guide to Design and Implementation*. San Francisco: Jossey-Bass, 2014, Kindle.

Merriam, Sharan B., and Elizabeth J. Tisdell. *Qualitative Research: A Guide to Design and Implementation* (4th ed.). San Francisco: Jossey-Bass, 2015.

Mertens, Donna M. *Research and Evaluation in Education and Psychology: Integrating Diversity with Quantitative, Qualitative, and Mixed Methods* (4th ed.) Thousand Oaks, CA: SAGE Publications, 2014.

Miles, Matthew B., A. Michael Huberman, and Johnny Saldaña. *Qualitative Data Analysis: A Methods Sourcebook* (3rd ed). Thousand Oaks, CA: SAGE Publications, 2018.

Moustakas, Clark. *Phenomenological Research Methods.* Thousand Oaks, CA: SAGE Publications, 1994.

Moylan, Carrie A., and McKenzie Javorka. "Widening the Lens: An Ecological Review of Campus Sexual Assault." *Trauma, Violence, & Abuse* 21, no. 1 (2020): 179-192.

Mundorf, Norbert, Mike Allen, David D'Alessio, and Tara M. Emmers-Sommer. "Effects of Sexually Explicit Media." In *Mass Media Effects Research: Advances Through Meta-Analysis,* 181-198. Mahwah, NJ: Lawrence Erlbaum Associates, 2007.

Nakkash, Rima T., Lilian A. Ghandour, Nasser Yassin, Sirine Anouti, Ali Chalak, Sara Chehab, Aida El-Aily, and Rima A. Afifi. "'Everyone Has the Right to Drink Beer': A Stakeholder Analysis of Challenges to Youth Alcohol Harm-Reduction Policies in Lebanon." *International Journal of Environmental Research and Public Health* 16, no. 16 (2019): 2874.

National Commission for the Protection of Human Subjects of Biomedical and Behavioral Research. 1979. *The Belmont Report: Ethical Principles and Guidelines for the Protection of Human Subjects of Research.* https://www.hhs.gov/ohrp/regulations-and-policy/belmont-report/read-the-belmont-report/index.html

National Institute of Justice. 2015. "Sexual Assault Kits: Using Science to Find Solutions." http://nij.gov/unsubmitted-kits/documents/unsubmitted-kits.pdf

National Sexual Violence Resource Center. 2018. "Statistics." https://www.nsvrc.org/statistics

O'Neal, Eryn Nicole. "Victim Cooperation in Intimate Partner Sexual Assault Cases: A Mixed Methods Examination." *Justice Quarterly* 34, no. 6 (2017): 1014-1043.

—. "'Victim is not credible': The influence of rape culture on police perceptions of sexual assault complainants." *Justice Quarterly* 36, no. 1 (2019): 127-160.

O'Neal, Eryn Nicole, and Brittany E. Hayes. "'A Rape is a Rape, Regardless of What the Victim Was Doing at the Time': Detective Views on How 'Problematic' Victims Affect Sexual Assault Case Processing." *Criminal Justice Review* 45, no. 1 (2020): 26-44.

Ogletree, Shirley Matile, Paulette Diaz, and Vincent Padilla. "What Is Feminism? College Students' Definitions and Correlates." *Current Psychology* 38, no. 6 (2019): 1576-1589.

Oktavina, Sinta. "Population Growth Control Policy and Its Effect to Law Enforcement." *Journal of Law and Legal Reform* 1, no. 2 (2020): 225-240.

Owusu, Mensah, Melissa Nursey-Bray, and Diane Rudd. "Gendered Perception and Vulnerability to Climate Change in Urban Slum Communities in Accra, Ghana." *Regional Environmental Change* 19, no. 1 (2019): 13-25.

Patton, Michael Q. *Qualitative Research and Evaluation Methods.* Thousand Oaks, CA: SAGE Publications, 2002.

Percy, William H., Kim Kostere, and Sandra Kostere. "Generic Qualitative Research in Psychology." *The Qualitative Report* 20, no. 2 (2015): 76-85.

Peterson, Joseph, Donald Johnson, Denise Herz, Lisa Graziano, and Taly Oehler. "Sexual Assault Kit Backlog Study." Washington, DC: The National Institute of Justice, 2012.

Pfeffer, Jeffrey, and Gerald Salancik. *External Control of Organizations—Resource Dependence Perspective.* New York: Routledge, 2015.

Pinchevsky, Gillian M. "Criminal Justice Considerations for Unsubmitted and Untested Sexual Assault Kits: A Review of the Literature and Suggestions for Moving Forward." *Criminal Justice Policy Review* 29, no. 9 (2018): 925-945.

Qiong, O. U. "A Brief Introduction to Perception." *Studies in Literature and Language* 15, no. 4 (2017): 18-28.

Quinlan, Andrea. "Visions of Public Safety, Justice, and Healing: The Making of the Rape Kit Backlog in the United States." *Social & Legal Studies* 29, no. 2 (2020): 225-245.

Rahi, Samar. "Research Design and Methods: A Systematic Review of Research Paradigms, Sampling Issues and Instruments Development." *International Journal of Economics & Management Sciences* 6, no. 2 (2017): 1-5.

Richards, L., and J. M. Morse. "The Integrity of Qualitative Research." In *Readme First for a User's Guide to Qualitative Methods*, 25-44. Thousand Oaks, CA: SAGE Publications, 2007.

Robinson, Oliver C. "Sampling in Interview-Based Qualitative Research: A Theoretical and Practical Guide." *Qualitative Research in Psychology* 11, no. 1 (2014): 25-41.

Sandhu, Ajay. "'I'm Glad That Was on Camera': A Case Study of Police Officers' Perceptions of Cameras." *Policing and Society* 29, no. 2 (2019): 223-235.

Sexual Violence Research Initiative. 2020. "Definitions." https://www.svri.org/research-methods/definitions

Shaw, Jessica, Rebecca Campbell, Debi Cain, and Hannah Feeney. "Beyond Surveys and Scales: How Rape Myths Manifest in Sexual Assault Police Records." *Psychology of Violence* 7, no. 4 (2017): 602-614.

Shelby, Renee. "Whose Rape Kit? Stabilizing the Vitullo® Kit Through Positivist Criminology and Protocol Feminism." *Theoretical Criminology* 24, no. 4 (2020): 669-688.

Shields, Stephanie A. "Functionalism, Darwinism, and Advances in the Psychology of Women and Gender: From the 19th Century to the 21st." *Feminism & Psychology* 26, no. 4 (2016): 397-404.

Sinclair, Guy Fiti. "The Original Sin (and Salvation) of Functionalism." *European Journal of International Law* 26, no. 4 (2015): 965-973.

Speaker, Paul J. "The Jurisdictional Return on Investment from Processing the Backlog of Untested Sexual Assault Kits." *Forensic Science International: Synergy* 1 (2019): 18-23.

Spohn, Cassia, and Katharine Tellis. "Sexual Assault Case Outcomes: Disentangling the Overlapping Decisions of Police and Prosecutors." *Justice Quarterly* 36, no. 3 (2019): 383-411.

Spohn, Cassia. "Sexual Assault Case Processing: The More Things Change, the More They Stay the Same." *International Journal for Crime, Justice and Social Democracy* 9, no. 1 (2020): 86-94.

Steiner, Gerald. "From Probabilistic Functionalism to a Mental Simulation of Innovation: By Collaboration from Vulnerabilities to Resilient Societal Systems." *Environment Systems and Decisions* 38, no. 1 (2018): 92-98.

Strom, Kevin J., and Matthew J. Hickman. "Untested Sexual Assault Kits: Searching for an Empirical Foundation to Guide Forensic Case Processing Decisions." *Criminology & Public Policy* 15 (2016): 593-601.

Susskind, Lawrence. "Comments on 'Managing Complexity: From Visual Perception to Sustainable Transitions. Contributions of Brunswik's Theory of Probabilistic Functionalism.'" *Environment Systems and Decisions* 38, no. 1 (2018): 74-75.

Swartout, Kevin M., William F. Flack Jr, Sarah L. Cook, Loreen N. Olson, Paige Hall Smith, and Jacquelyn W. White. "Measuring Campus Sexual Misconduct and Its Context: The Administrator-Researcher Campus Climate Consortium (ARC3) Survey." *Psychological Trauma: Theory, Research, Practice, and Policy* 11, no. 5 (2019): 495-504.

Swerdlow, Benjamin A., Jennifer G. Pearlstein, Devon B. Sandel, Iris B. Mauss, and Sheri L. Johnson. "Maladaptive Behavior and Affect Regulation: A Functionalist Perspective." *Emotion* 20, no. 1 (2020): 75-79.

Taylor, Erik C., Benjamin D. McLarty, and Dale A. Henderson. "The Fire Under the Gridiron: Resource Dependence and NCAA Conference Realignment." *Journal of Business Research* 82 (2018): 246-259.

Tessier, Sophie. "From Field Notes, to Transcripts, to Tape Recordings: Evolution or Combination?" *International Journal of Qualitative Methods* 11, no. 4 (2012): 446-460.

Thompson, Katherine M. "Helping Survivors of Sexual Assault." *Journal of the American Academy of PAs* 33, no. 1 (2020): 39-44.

Thompson, Paul, and David McHugh. "Work Organizations: A Critical Approach." *Organizational Memory. The Academy of Management Review* 16, no. 1 (2009): 57-91.

Tripathi, Bibha. "Feminist Criminology: Some Reflections." *Vidhigya: The Journal of Legal Awareness* 9, no. 1 (2014).

Tufford, Lea, and Peter Newman. "Bracketing in Qualitative Research." *Qualitative Social Work* 11, no. 1 (2012): 80-96.

Turner, S. G., & Maschi, T. M. (2015). "Feminist and Empowerment Theory and Social Work Practice." *Journal of Social Work Practice*, 29(2), 151-162.

U.S. Department of Justice. 2018. "Sexual Assault." https://www.justice.gov/ovw/sexual-assault

—. 2020. "Providing Victims of Sexual Assault the Care They Deserve." https://www.ojp.gov/news/ojp-blogs/2020-ojp-blogs/providing-victims-sexual-assault-care-they-deserve

—. n.d. "Sexual Assault Toolkit." https://www.ncjrs.gov/ovc_archives/sartkit/develop/comm-language-b.html

UNICEF. 2017. "Sexual Violence." https://data.unicef.org/topic/child-protection/violence/sexual-violence/

Valentine, Julie L., L. Kathleen Sekula, Lawrence J. Cook, Rebecca Campbell, Alison Colbert, and Victor W. Weedn. "Justice Denied: Low Submission Rates of Sexual Assault Kits and the Predicting Variables." *Journal of Interpersonal Violence* 34, no. 17 (2019): 3547-3573.

Van Brunt, Brian, Amy Murphy, Lisa Pescara-Kovach, and Gina-Lyn Crance. "Early Identification of Grooming and Targeting in Predatory Sexual Behavior on College Campuses." *Violence and Gender* 6, no. 1 (2019): 16-24.

Venema, Rachel M. "Making Judgments: How Blame Mediates the Influence of Rape Myth Acceptance in Police Response to Sexual Assault." *Journal of Interpersonal Violence* 34, no. 13 (2019): 2697-2722.

Walton, Douglas, and Nanning Zhang. "The Epistemology of Scientific Evidence." *Artificial Intelligence and Law* 21, no. 2 (2013): 173-219.

Wang, Can, and Lawrence M. Wein. "Analyzing Approaches to the Backlog of Untested Sexual Assault Kits in the USA." *Journal of Forensic Sciences* 63, no. 4 (2018): 1110-1121.

Ward, L. Monique, Ann Merriwether, and Allison Caruthers. "Breasts Are for Men: Media, Masculinity Ideologies, and Men's Beliefs About Women's Bodies." *Sex Roles* 55, no. 9-10 (2006): 703-714.

Wells, William. "Some Considerations When Making Decisions About Prioritizing Sexual Assault Kits for Forensic Testing." *Criminology & Public Policy* 15 (2016): 585.

Wells, William, Ashley K. Fansher, and Bradley A. Campbell. "The Results of CODIS-Hit Investigations in a Sample of Cases with Unsubmitted Sexual Assault Kits." *Crime & Delinquency* 65, no. 1 (2019): 122-148.

Wentzlof, Chloe A., Jaimie E. Kerka, James H. Albert, Jon E. Sprague, and Lewis O. Maddox. "Comparison of Decision Tree and Logistic Regression Models for Utilization in Sexual Assault Kit Processing." *Journal of Forensic Sciences* 64, no. 2 (2019): 528-533.

Whalley, Elizabeth. "The 'Bait and Switch' of Sexual Assault Response: Expanded Carceral Power at a Rape Crisis Center." *Affilia* 35, no. 2 (2020): 200-217.

World Health Organization. 2012. "Understanding and Addressing Violence Against Women." https://www.who.int/reproductivehealth/topics/violence/vaw_series/en/

World Population Review. 2020. "Rape Statistics by Country 2020." https://worldpopulationreview.com/countries/rape-statistics-by-country/

World Resource Institute. 2017. "WRI 2017 Funding Commitments."
    https://www.wri.org/about/wri-2017-funding-commitments

Worrall, John L., and Jihong Zhao. "The Role of the COPS Office in
    Community Policing." *Policing: An International Journal of Police
    Strategies & Management* 26, no. 1 (2003): 64-87.

Wright, Paul J., and Michelle Funk. "Pornography Consumption and
    Opposition to Affirmative Action for Women: A Prospective
    Study." *Psychology of Women Quarterly* 38, no. 2 (2014): 208-221.

Wright, Paul J., and Robert S. Tokunaga, R. *Men's Objectifying Media
    Consumption, Objectification of Women, and Attitudes Supportive of
    Violence Against Women.* New York: Science & Business Media, 2015.

Zacks, Jeffrey M. "Event Perception and Memory." *Annual Review of
    Psychology* 71 (2020): 165-191.